Proportionalism

PROPORTIONALISM

The American Debate and its European Roots

BERNARD HOOSE

GEORGETOWN UNIVERSITY PRESS

Library of Congress Cataloging-in-Publication Data
Hoose, Bernard.

   Proportionalism: the American debate and its
European roots.

   Bibliography: p.
   Includes index.
     1. Christian ethics—Catholic authors.   2. Christian
ethics—United States—History—20th century.
3. Catholic Church—Doctrines—History—20th century.
I. Title.

BJ1249.H59   1987   241'.042   87-8357
ISBN 0-87840-454-6
ISBN 0-87840-455-4 (pbk.)

Der Fuchs

I have seen the fox at work beneath the Roman sky,
Patient in his hunt for truth, astute, but never sly.
An over eager cub could drive a saint around the bend,
But I have seen the fox as both a teacher and a friend.

Contents

Preface

A most interesting and, at times, even fiery debate in the realm of moral theology has attracted an enormous amount of attention in the English-speaking world and more particularly in the United States over the last fifteen years or so. As it deals with the very essence of behavioral norms, it is of no small import, and only a fool could dismiss it as just one more of those learned discussions which are of interest to academics but have little or nothing to do with real life. The debate in question deals with what has come to be known as proportionalism.

Over the centuries, proportionate reason has, quite naturally, played a central role in a number of principles employed in Catholic moral theology, as, for example, the principle of double effect, the principle of the lesser of two evils, and, in more recent times, the principle of totality. In insisting upon its centrality, those present-day theologians who are known as proportionalists could be said to be merely developing something which has always been in our tradition. It could, then, be thought that their theories are neither exciting nor revolutionary. However, the proportionalists point out that the centrality of proportionate reason was not always sufficiently recognized in the past and that much more emphasis was often put on other factors, such as, for example, the directness or indirectness of the act. The implications of the writings of these theologians are therefore of enormous importance. If what they say about the centrality of proportionate reason is true, much of what has been said in the past about so-called deontological norms loses some of its sense, while the traditional distinction between acts which are described as direct and those which are described as indirect needs a certain amount of revision.

Proportionalism had its beginnings in Europe, but the amount of attention it has attracted in that continent varies considerably from one country to another. A large quantity of literature on the subject has been produced in Germany, for example, while in Italy, although a certain amount has been written, one could not say that there is enough to plunge readers of Italian journals into what might be called an Italian debate on proportionalism. If we look across the Atlantic, however, we find that proportionalism has attracted enormous interest among theologians and philosophers in the United States, and that interest—which, as we shall see, has not always been favorable—has not been confined to the ranks of Roman Catholicism, although the debate itself is generally considered to be a Catholic one. Within a few years of its importation, proportionalism had attracted many American adherents, and a wealth of literature has been published on the subject in the English language over the past fifteen years or so. A debate, of course, usually involves some opposition, and that is precisely the case here. The opposition comes from a number of scholars who insist on the importance of deontological norms of behavior and fear that, in proportionalism, the concept of intrinsic evil is in danger of being relativized. The vehemence with which some have expressed their opposition has served to emphasize how important an issue proportionalism is. Moreover, although there have been a number of misunderstandings, the quality of the opposition and the need to reply to it have brought about significant developments in the debate. However, although articles and books concerning the subject continue to roll off the presses, and although there is obviously a genuine searching, a certain number of trenches seem to have been dug, or, if I may be allowed to change the metaphor, it would seem that a situation of stalemate has been reached.

It has often been said that, unless we know the history of a country or of a field of study, we cannot understand the present situation in that country or field of study, and neither can we plan future steps wisely; and future steps would, of course, include moving out of a situation of impasse. The debate on proportionalism in the United States is no exception. It is, perhaps, not surprising that no history of that debate has yet appeared, when one considers the period of time involved. However, without a more historical approach than anything we have seen so far, how can we hope to acquire the necessary light for future steps? The present work aims to fill that lacuna. If proportionalism attracted much attention in the United States, there must have been a reason, or, more likely, reasons. What were those reasons? There were certain developments. What were they? Why and how did they take place? There were problems. There was opposition. Why? What was involved? Was the opposition justified? Were any problems resolved? How? In this work I have attempted to shed light on these problematic areas.

Although I have spoken of history, I cannot and will not pretend that the present work is a mere record of facts. In order to get as near as possible to the cores of the various problems, I have indulged in discussions with various scholars here and there throughout the text, and have also suggested ways out of apparent impasse situations. The concluding section in each chapter, except the first, is dedicated to indicating how much light has been thrown on problem areas in the preceding sections. In view of the fact that a number of articles written by Europeans were translated into English and published in the United States, we may consider them to be part of the debate that has been going on in North America and, to a much lesser degree, in other parts of the English-speaking world. However, I have also found that certain lacunae which appear here and there in the American debate can be filled by European works which have never been translated into English. Where mention is made of any of these works in the present volume, the lack of an English translation is indicated either in the main text or in a footnote. In order to explain the background to certain points, I have also drawn on some British philosophical works and one or two other English language sources.

The simplest approach to a work of this kind would seem to be the chronological one. However, such an approach would probably drive the reader to the furthest extremes of boredom. It would, moreover, be very difficult for the reader to keep in touch with the various problems. Problem "X," for example, might be raised first, followed by problems "Y" and "Z." After "Z," "X" appears on the scene again, followed by problems "A" and "B." Then "Y" is picked up again. Problem "X" returns ten years later, and so on. To avoid these problems of utter confusion and sheer boredom, I have dedicated each chapter, except the final one, to a particular sphere. The first two chapters serve as an introduction to the whole subject, and deal with such questions as: what were the origins of proportionalism in general and in the United States in particular? what gave rise to it? how was it possible? was it needed?, etc. In order to deal in an orderly fashion with the various problems that arose in the debate over the years, I have divided among the third, fourth and fifth chapters the three main spheres in which these problems are found.

The first of these spheres—and the subject of the third chapter—is that of the rightness/goodness distinction. Goodness here refers to the moral goodness of the person. Rightness, on the other hand, refers to the correctness of the action, whether it be performed by a morally good person or by a morally bad one. We shall see that an enormous amount of confusion between these two concepts on both sides of the debate has certainly not made it easy for people to understand what proportionalism is.

The fourth chapter deals with the sphere of the teleology/deontology distinction. Much of the inspiration for a number of the points raised in the debate came from Anglo-Saxon philosophy. That much is undoubted. Sometimes, however, upon reading certain works, one could be forgiven for thinking that the debate on proportionalism is just a part or extension of the philosophical debate between teleologists and deontologists in Great Britain, the United States, and other parts of the English-speaking world, with the utilitarian G.E. Moore on the side of the proportionalists and W.D. Ross defending the cause of the Catholic deontologists. This is very odd indeed when one considers the fact that the proportionalists are most certainly not utilitarians, and W.D. Ross is not a deontologist in anything like the sense that is given to that word in Catholic moral theology circles. To explain just how this strange state of affairs came to exist and still persists is one of the aims of the third chapter. We shall also see how, in fact, proportionalism developed as something quite different from utilitarianism or consequentialism.

The third and final problem area is that of the direct/indirect distinction. Disagreement regarding the usefulness or otherwise of this particular distinction centers for the most part on the concept of intrinsic evil. This is dealt with in the fifth chapter, where we shall see that the adoption of a more teleological approach to norms of behavior on the part of the proportionalists was not enough to remove all polemics regarding the direct/indirect distinction.

In short, then, in the third, fourth and fifth chapters we trace, analyze, question and comment upon the development (or lack of development) of themes, rather than describe a sequence of articles and books. Then in the final chapter we see what can be gathered from the preceding chapters so that light may be thrown on the present situation. In examining both sides of a debate in this way, a researcher is naturally influenced by what he reads and analyzes. The reader will see that the present writer has found himself disagreeing with participants on both sides of the debate on various points. It will be clear, however, that, if labels must be applied, then I must be labelled a proportionalist. My reasons for being so inclined will, I think, be evident from my comments not only in the concluding chapter, but throughout the work.

CHAPTER ONE

How It Began

In the early years of the debate that we are about to discuss, the term "proportionalism" was not used.[1] There was simply a movement among certain theologians to show the decisive role played by proportionate reason in moral decision making. One writer spoke of a preference axiom[2] but his reasoning was very similar to that of his colleagues and so he too was later branded as a "proportionalist" along with them. The theologian who is generally considered to have started the movement which came to be known as proportionalism was a young German called Peter Knauer, whose first contribution appeared in 1965.[3] As it was written in French, we may assume that the article did not have a very wide readership in the United States, or, indeed, in the rest of the Anglo-Saxon world, until a somewhat reduced English language version was published two years later. However, the basic ideas of the article no doubt reached many through McCormick's review of it in his widely read "Notes on Moral Theology" in *Theological Studies*.[4]

1. A Start but not a Start

The work of a young student, Knauer's first article was a remarkable achievement. Unfortunately, however, it is not easily understood, and there can be little doubt that some of the early misunderstandings can be traced to that one simple fact. Let us therefore attempt to state his case in somewhat simpler terms than those used by him. Knauer was of the opinion that the standard interpretations of the principle of double effect caused many problems. He was also uneasy about the fragmentation of the human act into unreal parts that seemed normal in those interpretations. He pointed out that in St. Thomas' definition of self-defense— which, rightly or wrongly, he saw as the beginning of the principle of double effect[5]—the term "effect" is not used merely as a correlative to "cause." The term "aspect" would better fit what Thomas wished to say.

1

Having thus interpreted Aquinas, Knauer lined up behind him, preferring to speak of two aspects of one and the same action, rather than two effects, thus safeguarding the unity of the human act.[6] Although he was critical of the standard interpretations, however, Knauer was not inclined to pronounce the principle of double effect defunct. Instead, he described it as the fundamental principle of all morality.[7] But Knauer's version of that principle was a somewhat reduced one: "The moral subject may permit an evil effect of his act only if this effect is indirect, being counterbalanced by a proportionate reason."[8]

In the last analysis, he maintained, all moral evil is defined by its mediate or immediate relation to a "physical" or ontological evil (such as, for example, sickness or error). For Knauer, the morally good is what he calls the "simply good." By that he means the ontological (or physical) good of any reality.[9] But what if a certain physical good (health, for example) cannot be achieved without the production of a physical evil (e.g., a loss of fertility in the patient)? Such a good is morally good, says Knauer, only if the physical evil associated with it is objectively beyond the intention of the person willing. If that is the case, it is the simply good that determines the intention. If, however, the evil is intended, the act is morally evil. Evil is intended, continues Knauer, if the permitting or causing of it is not justified by a proportionate reason. That is, the act does not correspond to its reason (its end). For St. Thomas, he says, "what remains outside the intention" is "accidental": "When the dairy-maid churns, she necessarily obtains some buttermilk as a by-product, even without having that intention: whilst being necessary, this effect may remain accidental to the intention of making butter."[10]

Sin, says Knauer, consists in allowing an evil without a proportionate reason. In such a case, the evil is not "accidental"; it enters into the very object of one's act. If, however, there is a proportionate reason for allowing an evil effect, that evil effect becomes indirect. A bad effect (or aspect) will be direct or indirect depending on the presence or absence of a proportionate reason. The difference between direct and indirect, therefore, is not formally a physical difference.[11] The reason, moreover, is not exterior to the act, but cooperates in the constitution of the *finis operis* (i.e., the end of the act). However, that does not make the bad aspects of the act indirect. After all, he asks, is it not true that we have a good reason for all our acts? These bad effects can enter into the direct object of the act and be formally willed. They will not be willed for themselves, of course, but on account of the good to which they are linked. For the bad effects to become indirect, the good reason must occupy the entire field of the direct object of the act, so that the direct object is fully identified with the good reason of that same act. In other words, the proportionate reason is nothing other than the direct object. It is the *finis operis* of the act, which, when a proportionate reason exists, coincides with the good effect or aspect.[12] As some values appear to be incommensurable, how can we work out whether or not a reason is proportionate? The real criterion of proportionate reason, says Knauer, is the proportion of the act to its end; there is proportion when the act is proportioned to the value being pursued.[13]

In this article Knauer was not careful to distinguish between personal moral goodness/evil and the moral rightness or wrongness of an act. As will become clear in Chapter Three, this distinction was much discussed later in the debate, and is regarded as enormously important by the present author. Such, however, was not the attitude of Richard McCormick in 1966, it would seem. He reviewed Knauer's article very shortly after its publication, and his reaction to it was not, on the whole, very favorable, but for reasons other than the one I have just mentioned. Knauer had written that, in a medical operation involving the removal of an obstacle to produce a cure, it could happen "accidentally" that the obstacle is a member of the organism. In such a case the removal of the member would not be willed directly because it is justified by a proportionate reason. McCormick suggested that we could change the wording a little and say that the obstacle could "accidentally" be a living nonviable fetus, and that, in such a case, the removal of the fetus would not be willed directly because it would be justified by a proportionate reason. "One senses immediately," he says, "that something is wrong here."[14]

That, moreover, was not the only problem for McCormick.

> If applied right down the line, this reasoning would destroy the concept of that which is intrinsically evil *ex objecto*. Knauer might disown this conclusion. But it is not clear to me that he could do so logically. Of course, his formulation is not necessarily wanting because it leads to such conclusions (for we cannot exclude the possibility that the conclusions are correct); it is vulnerable only if in doing so it proves inconsistent. I believe this is the case.[15]

Knauer, he says, makes it theoretically possible for any means to be indirect and licit providing it is necessary to an envisaged value or end. McCormick does not see how, if he applied his own principles, Knauer could conclude (as he did) that to kill in order to obtain money was murder. Knauer would have to claim that the motive or reason was not proportionate, but that could be questioned. He suggests that, following Knauer's line of thinking, one could conclude that it is licit to destroy one million enemy civilians (noncombatants) by people bombing as an effective deterrent against the loss of five million American lives. These deaths, says McCormick, would, in Knauer's terms, be indirect because of the existence of a proportionate reason.[16]

McCormick later became the champion of proportionalism in the United States. Why then, we may ask, was his review of Knauer's first article on the subject so very unfavorable? Part of the answer, I think, is to be found elsewhere in the same edition of his "Notes," where he discusses D.F. O'Callaghan's thoughts on the subject of spies taking their own lives in order to protect their comrades.[17] Agreeing with O'Callaghan that such action is illicit, he writes that, although the revelation of secret information under torture could cause harm to other people, he doubts that this probability puts the captured spy in the category of unjust aggressor. It must be assumed that, in using human agents with such limits, governments understand the risks involved and accept them. He admits that "the indirect voluntary leaves us scratching our heads at times," but he thinks it is capable of dealing with the "vast majority of sacrificial vs. suicidal situations." For that reason he prefers to go along with it even if an unpopular solution results, if that solution constitutes the only reason for abandoning it.[18]

The physically direct killing of a fetus has, of course, much in common with the physically direct killing of oneself. It may well be that one of McCormick's difficulties lay in the fact that the fetus, like the spy, could not be put into the category of unjust aggressor. Another difficulty was caused by his tendency in this article to interpret "proportion" as a mathematical term. For Knauer, proportion is lacking when the act performed undermines the very value being pursued. The protection of innocent life by the unnecessary destruction of innocent life would surely, on those terms, *not* be proportionate, because it involves an undermining of the value being pursued.

McCormick also wrote that Knauer had failed to distinguish proportionate reasons which are identical to the good effect produced immediately by the cause from proportionate reasons which are motives " 'introduced from outside,' so to speak, and superimposed on an external act whose basic meaning is already determined (because of its unique immediate effect)."[19] However, as Knauer himself later pointed out, he had referred to this distinction as that between the *finis operis* and the *finis operantis* (i.e., the end of the person acting), the latter being the *finis operis* of a second act.[20]

A certain amount of McCormick's difficulties at this time may have arisen from mere misunderstandings. He himself later referred to Knauer's second article as a substantial clarification, and was much more appreciative of that "revised version."[21] It is also worth bearing in mind, however, that, much later, he declared that he had been led by colleagues to several changes of mind on important subjects in the period from 1965 to 1980, as a result of the influences to which he had been subject in writing his "Notes on Moral Theology."[22] From a proportionalist's point of view, then, the McCormick of the mid 1960s was perhaps something of a conservative, but so, it would seem, were the vast majority of his colleagues at that time.

Although Knauer's first article was read by some American theologians and did bear some fruit,[23] it would, I think, be an exaggeration to claim that his brand of proportionalism had any kind of firm foothold in the United States before the publication of Paul VI's encyclical *Humanae Vitae,* and even, perhaps, for some time afterwards.

2. A New Beginning Made Possible

American theology has perhaps always tended to rely heavily on European thought.[24] It would, however, be naive to think that proportionalism gained ground in the United States merely because American theologians accepted uncritically what their German and other European colleagues told them. There were reasons for the appearance and development of proportionalism in the United States, and it is those reasons that we must now examine if we wish to attain a deep understanding and appreciation of the debate and the road that it has taken over the past two decades.

(a) *Problems for the Moral Theologians*   In the 1960s the Catholic Church was taking a stand against the liberalizing attitudes toward abortion which were coming to the fore in several countries. Within that church itself, however, there was a certain amount of debate regarding the more restricted arena of the so-called therapeutic abortion. At that time Catholic theology did, of course, allow the killing of innocent persons for a proportionate reason in instances where the killing was described as "indirect." We may take as an instance of this the case of a pregnant woman suffering from cancer of the uterus. The cancer is spreading, and unless a surgeon intervenes, it will bring about the deaths of both mother and baby. If, however, the uterus is removed, the mother's life will be saved, although the fetus (an innocent person) will die in the process. Such a killing would have been justified by the traditional principle of double effect. The same principle could have been applied in the case of an ectopic pregnancy where the embryo was developing in the fallopian tube. In view of the fact that the tube was the problem inasmuch as it was pathological, doctors would have been allowed to cut it out, the intention being to cure the pathology.[25] All this was very clear and very tidy, but then new possibilities became apparent.

> Lately, some theologians have maintained that the doctor does not have to wait for the tube to rupture. The blood of the tube is already being infected by the fetus and is thus pathological before the rupture occurs. Thus one may remove the tube with the fetus in it before the tube ruptures.
>
> But here a further question must also be raised. What if the doctor can interfere by removing the fetus without taking out the tube? If the doctor has to remove the tube too, then the chances of the woman's giving birth again are greatly reduced. By removing just the fetus, the doctor does not impair the childbearing ability of the mother. The doctor knows that the fetus has no chance to live and sooner or later will have to be removed. The logical solution would be to remove the fetus and save the tube if possible.[26]

Could it be possible that the doctor should choose the method which causes the most damage (i.e., cut out the tube)? Many theologians began to think not.[27]

We have already had reason to touch upon the subject of killing oneself. Not long after McCormick had expressed his opinion on the matter in the article referred to above, somewhat different opinions were beginning to be aired. Cornelius Van der Poel, for instance, noted that, if there are five men on a raft which can safely hold only four, one of the men can jump off and swim away. Although he is certain to die, his death is indirect. However, continues Van der Poel, some moralists would not permit the self-killing of a prisoner of war who knows the whereabouts of 500 men behind enemy lines and wishes to prevent the enemy from brainwashing him and thereby discovering the whereabouts of those men. "Such tragic human situations seem to indicate the fallacy of determining morality merely on the physical structure of the act itself."[28]

Killing onself in very unusual circumstances may be considered by some theologians to be of mainly academic interest in discussions about ethics, and of little importance on the practical level. Not so the subject of artificial contraception, however. In a book published toward the end of 1964, W. Van der Marck noted that a scholarly bibliography just for that year included, at the time of writing, over one hundred items. From all sides, he said, the traditional point of view was being criticized.[29] In an introduction to the English language version of the same book, Lawrence Bright probably summed up rather well the feelings of many people throughout the world. The Catholic, he said, was often puzzled by the very moral prohibitions that he accepted.

> Just why mechanical contraception is out while the use of the infertile period (rhythm) is in, is not easy to grasp. The common answer that rhythm is more natural, is odd in view of the need for careful thermometer readings or consultations of the almanac.[30]

In the United States, John Noonan made some interesting observations. The church, he said, was on a pilgrim path. On her journey along that path she had grown in grace and wisdom. It had once been the common opinion of theologians that intercourse should be only for procreation, that intercourse during menstruation was mortal sin, that it was forbidden to have intercourse during pregnancy, and that there was a natural position for intercourse. "Was the commitment to an absolute prohibition of contraception more conscious, more universal, more complete, than to these now obsolete rules?" We could regard these now superseded opinions, he went on, as attempts to preserve basic values in the light of the biological data which was available at that time, as well as in the context of the challenges which were made to the Christian view of man at that time.[31]

The problem of divorce and remarriage is perhaps one of the best-known aspects of American society, largely as a result of the immense amount of publicity given to relationships among people involved in the entertainment industry. The problem apparently has appalling dimensions, even among Catholics. Although exact statistics are not available for this last mentioned group, Lawrence G. Wrenn estimates that in 1971 "something like 120,000" presumably valid Catholic marriages ended in civil divorces.[32] In that very year appeared the English version of an article which perhaps better than most reflected the feelings of many would-be revisionists. It was originally written in French and was translated for the

British magazine, *Clergy Review*. The author J.P. Jossua, raises a number
of points. If, he asks, separation is often the best solution to marriage
problems, why should remarriage be refused? He sees the value of faithful
love as a sign, but points out that separation renders that sign null. A
person can give a sign of faith by renouncing another marriage, but, he
adds, that person no longer gives a sign of love. Although he admits that
"indissolubility as a sign is both a demand and a grace," Jossua feels that
foregoing it might sometimes be the lesser evil.[33] As for Christ's precept
not to tear apart what God has put together, Jossua says that there is no
indication that Christ was saying that man does not have the power to
dissolve a marriage. What he did say is that man does not have such a
right.[34] Jossua does not feel that we can deduce from the biblical texts
that, when a dissolution occurs, one has a positive right to remarry. He
does, however, feel that "the present state of affairs is intolerable."[35] The
Latin and Greek Fathers, as well as the fifth and sixth century councils,
clearly thought that marriage was dissolved by persistent adultery, and
there is "plenty of testimony" that remarriage, while not being a right,
was tolerated for the innocent party. This practice, which has continued
in the Orthodox Church, could be taken as a starting point. Perhaps the
ecclesial status of a second marriage could be recognized "by means of a
positive act receiving the partners back into communion."[36]

Writing in 1966, B. Peters, T. Beemer and C. Van der Poel discussed
the problem of cohabitation after the breakdown of a first marriage. They
were convinced

> that there can be very real circumstances because of which *certain* persons
> who live in such co-habitation in a marital state of mind can be morally
> justified before God and before the Church because they *cannot* live in any
> other way because of the imperfection in which a man of goodwill sometimes
> *must* live.[37]

By the time proportionalism had become a noticeable factor in American
moral theology, however, Curran was surely not the only American theologian who felt that an adequate solution to the problem is not provided
by keeping the present teaching on indissolubility and making changes
in theological and legal understandings so that more marriages may be
declared invalid. Accepting the absolute teaching on indissolubility but
introducing a pastoral toleration of second marriages after divorce is also
inadequate and can only be a temporary move which must go further.
"In the light of the self understanding of moral theology today, perspec-

tives and reasons have been proposed for changing the teaching of the Church on indissolubility."[38]

(b) *Attempts to Deal with the Problems*   Numerous moralists attempted to deal with these problems.[39] Some of them helped to prepare the ground for proportionalism by the questions they raised, the conclusions they came to and even by the mistakes that they made. One such moralist was W. Van der Marck. Writing in the same year in which Knauer produced his first article, Van der Marck took up the problem of artificial contraception. The prevailing view regarding progesterones, he said, was that their use was either therapeutic or sterilizing/contraceptive. Why were there no other legitimate possibilities for their use, such as, for example, controlling fertility or making possible the expression of mutual love without an immediate pregnancy resulting? "We begin to suspect," he declared, "that the famous principle of the act with a double effect is responsible for all such dilemmas."[40] Against the view that there could be such uses for progesterones a difficulty is raised as follows: "The purpose or intention of one's act, as stated above, may very well be good in itself, but it can be achieved only with the help of *bad means*."[41]

There is, however, a fundamental error in this way of thinking, says Van der Marck, and that error lies in the fact that we are giving a separate existence and moral significance to the physical or physiological element. Two human acts may be *externally* and *materially* much the same, and yet one may be entirely different from the other. Examples of this would be murder and the execution of a criminal, or mutilation and transplantation.[42]

> The real (formal) difference between acts which are externally (materially) completely alike arises from the essentially inter-subjective character of all human acts . . . The most fundamental and ultimate thing that can be said about a human act is that it is community-forming or community-breaking—it makes for a communal relationship, or rejects it.[43]

With all that, Van der Marck is not saying that the end (intention) lies spatially outside the means (act). Neither, he says, is it realized later on (temporally). It indicates what the human significance and meaning of the means (act) are. What we are concerned with, he continues, is the immanent finality of the material act within the sphere of intersubjectivity. A physical killing, for example, is, in its human significance, either community building or community destroying. It is justice or it is vengeance. In its human significance, physical mutilation is either communicative or community breaking: transplantation or mutilation.[44]

It is therefore nonsense, he says, to speak of bad means and good ends or good means and good ends. "Only the concrete human act is good or bad."[45] Van der Marck concludes from all this that a human act does not have a double effect. We can only say that an act such as mutilation has a double effect if the physical act alone "is considered as a *human* effect." That would be incorrect. We must therefore say that there is "only one effect, one human act: transplantation."[46]

In the case of a therapeutic abortion, if doctors decide that it is medically necessary to remove the fetus, and it is humanly acceptable to do so, then that removal is not abortion, "except perhaps in purely medical or phys- iological terms." Thus, he says, the principle that abortion is murder still applies.[47]

There were, of course, a number of questions left unanswered by Van der Marck. Even supposing that the existence of so many moral dilemmas was to be attributed to an unreal splitting of the human act into various good or bad components, can we say that he had really found a solution? How was one to decide that killing a fetus was medically necessary, that killing this criminal was an exercise of justice while killing that other criminal was murder, that telling an untruth in this case would be wrong but in that case would be right? How do we work out that something is community building or community destroying? These questions (enor- mously important ones) were still to be answered. Van der Marck, how- ever, had already taken strides along a road that went in the general direction of proportionalism. He had challenged the attitude that it was possible to describe an act (means) as wrong regardless of end and cir- cumstances. To say that it was wrong to speak of an act with a double effect was, perhaps, a little puzzling to some people. After all, some morally right acts do cause pain or loss or whatever. Clearly, if Van der Marck had made the same use as Knauer of the concept of physical or ontological evil, he could have avoided that problem. However, the point he wished to make was that the act is one. It is, for example, *either* transplantation *or* senseless mutilation.

Another interesting contribution came from the pen of Peter Chirico, who pointed out that we are sometimes faced by situations in which the various strands of moral law are so interwoven that the performance of one imperative makes the performance of another morally impossible. In such circumstances, he says, the Christian should recognize all the values involved. This he or she does by implementing all of them insofar as this is possible. This solution, he says, conforms with the absolutist position and holds that there are absolute moral norms which hold both *in abstracto* and *in concreto*. The infringement of these norms is always wrong because conscious infringement always involves moral harm to persons. Chirico also holds that his position agrees with that of the situationist in that it holds that there are cases in which a person may contravene absolutes. However, this contravention is not allowed because the imperatives have lost their validity in this particular case. Rather it is allowed because the person finds himself in a moral dilemma "in which he is incapable of living up to all the imperatives of the moral law." Although there are aspects of it that contravene moral absolutes, the act is subjectively without blame. However, the agent must recognize these evil aspects as such if he or she is to minimize the evil done.[48]

In reviewing this article, McCormick found problems. It seemed, from Chirico's use of words like "immoral" and "morally evil elements" that he thought that, unless all possible values are achieved by an act, the act is morally evil, in the sense that it contains morally evil elements. It would seem, said McCormick, that Chirico is measuring the objective moral quality of an act by its relation to a particular value. It seemed to him, however, that the moral specification should be derived from the relation of the act to the whole hierarchy of values.[49]

I would add here that Chirico, like so many other people (not surprisingly at that stage) had failed to grasp the importance of the distinctions between premoral evil, the moral wrongness of an act and the moral badness of the person acting. An act is either morally right or morally wrong. It cannot be both. If we talk of morally evil (meaning morally wrong) elements in an act that is morally right and is performed by a morally good person, we confuse the whole issue. We shall discuss such matters in much greater depth in Chapter Three.

The third writer we need to discuss is Charles Curran. In 1968 he expounded, in very few lines, his now famous theory (later called theology) of compromise. He underlined the fact that sin pervades the very atmosphere we live in and is in the very structures of human society. Sometimes the very best we can do is compromise, says Curran. In certain situations, the only way to survive is to perform an act (e.g., cheat in an exam in which everyone else is cheating) which, in more ideal circumstances, we would disapprove of.

From one point of view the act is good because it is the best that one can do. However, from the other aspect, the act is wrong and shows the presence of sin in the given situation which the Christian is continually called upon to overcome.[50]

We shall need to return to Curran's theory in a later chapter. For the time being, suffice it to note that he did well to highlight a problem (which, as we shall see, was later tackled by proportionalists), but that his own theory, as McCormick pointed out,[51] is not a theory or principle at all, because it does not tell us which compromise it is reasonable to make. I would add that, if an act is good (by which Curran evidently means right), it cannot also be wrong. Such use of terminology does not make for clarity. Rather, it is almost certain to provoke misunderstandings.

A principle presented for examination by Archbishop Denis Hurley in 1966 provoked similar criticism to that made about Curran's theory. The principle was stated very simply: "When the infringement of an obligation is necessarily involved in the exercise of a proportionate right, the obligation ceases. I call this the principle of the overriding right."[52]

Archbishop Hurley had perhaps had an insight into the fact that the deciding factor in judgments of moral rightness or wrongness has something to do with proportion, but his analysis did not go deep enough. McCormick pointed out that this principle merely states that, if one duty is more important than the other with which it clashes, then we should perform the more important one. It does not tell us how to work out which duty is the more important.[53] I would add here that the use of the word "duty" can be misleading if it is not qualified in any way. Duty is what one should do. W. D. Ross's expression *prima facie duty* would, I think, be better here.

By 1968 there were signs of a change in McCormick's own thought. The human significance of an action, he wrote at that time, tells us whether it is an action which promotes our neighbor's good or is an attack. Moral norms are just generalizations about the meaning or significance of actions. Moral significance is determined by relationship to personal value. He gives the example of the use of expressive powers, the meaning and purpose of which, we have come to see through reflection, "is not simply the communication of true information, but a communication between persons that respects and promotes their good precisely as persons in community." In determining whether or not a certain concrete act contains the malice of a lie, we need to keep in mind this overall purpose.

Spoken untruths are, at times, protective of, and even demanded by, personal values, while material truth sometimes destroys the values that veracity is meant to protect. He concludes that, rather than referring to mere physical acts, moral significance "is an assessment of an action's relation to the order of persons, to the hierarchy of personal value."[54]

McCormick went on to confront one of the problems we discussed earlier, and here we see clear signs of a change in his thinking. Previously, he had seen the self-killing of a spy as the direct killing of a nonaggressor (an innocent person, in other words). In 1968, but a little later than the article we have been discussing, he addressed himself to the problem of abortion. There has been in the course of time, he said, a constant sharpening and delimiting of the category of abortion. Contemporary formulations hinge on the concepts of "direct" and "innocent." Innocence seems to have been defined in relationship to the injustice involved in war, aggression and capital offenses, and the conclusion was that only in such cases of injustice was it morally tolerable to kill a person directly.

> Therefore, abortion is seen as an act whose basic moral quality is determined within the justice-injustice category.
>
> If, however, one distills from the three examples of morally tolerable killing a more general *ratio* (sc. that behind justice-injustice is a more general category, sc., *higher personal value*) then abortion as a form of forbidden killing might be recognised as that not justified by the hierarchy of personal value.[55]

Greater changes were to come, of course, in McCormick's thinking, but we shall have ample opportunity to discuss his later thought in other chapters. In the meantime, we shall turn to three other factors which helped to prepare the ground for proportionalism in the United States. Rather than factors, perhaps it would be better to describe them as three areas of movement in thought. The three areas concerned were: the magisterium, the specificity of Christian ethics and the natural law.

(c) *New Ideas about the Magisterium*   Although it is probable that most theologians who became involved in the debate about the magisterium in the late 1960s and early 1970s regretted the sensationalism and rather unacademic atmosphere that sometimes surrounded the discussion (perhaps too tranquil a word to describe what took place) between Hans Küng and the Vatican on this subject,[56] there was a growing feeling in theological circles that Catholic teaching on such matters as infallibility and dissent in the moral arena was not as clear as many might have thought. Pius XII had admitted in *Humani Generis* (1950) that pontiffs do not exercise their full doctrinal authority in encyclicals, but had added in the same paragraph that, when a pope makes a declaration on a subject which up to that time has been controversial, it must be clear to everybody that it is his intention that theologians should no longer freely debate that subject.[57] It does seem, moreover, that from the time of the declaration of papal infallibility at the First Vatican Council until the Second, there was a tendency among Catholic theologians, when dealing with the documents of the ordinary noninfallible magisterium, to limit themselves to saying how they thought the pontiff's words should be interpreted. As Mc-Cormick puts it, "they tended to be almost exegetical in their approach to these teachings and it was close to unthinkable (and certainly very risky) to question the formulation of such documents."[58]

In the postconciliar period, however, attitudes changed remarkably. At the council, changes had been made to teachings which had been authoritatively declared by the magisterium. It would, for instance, be more than difficult to hold that the declaration on religious liberty was in complete harmony with all previous statements from the magisterium on the subject. And then, of course, there was no hiding the fact that theologians who had been out of favor a few years before the council were back in favor during and after it (and not because they had retracted their views in the meantime).[59]

By 1968 (but before the publication of *Humanae Vitae*), the Archbishop of Westminster was wondering whether theologians would treat an encyclical with any more respect than they would an article in the magazine *Concilium*.[60] Whatever be the truth of that, by the time *Humanae Vitae* appeared on bookshelves, the relationship between theological research and the magisterium had developed into what McCormick described as "one of the most delicate theological problems surrounding discussion of the non-infallible moral magisterium."[61] And, of course, the appearance of *Humanae Vitae* only served to make the existence of the problems more evident and the solutions more urgent.

Taking *Humanae Vitae* as an example of a papal document which possibly contains error, Joseph Komonchak pointed out that we do not undermine papal teaching authority by holding that in one case or another, even a very serious case, it has been mistaken. Some might object that, if papal teaching on artificial contraception is wrong, then a very serious doctrinal error has been taught for centuries. Some theologians, he wrote, believe that the Holy Spirit cannot permit the church to fall into such serious error. However, one can say in reply that predicting how much evil God might permit to enter into the church is a very risky business. The church has been wrong a number of times in the past, and we have no a priori grounds on which to demonstrate that it could not be wrong again.[62]

Another point made by Komonchak is that it cannot be demonstrated a priori that it is not the Holy Spirit who is leading people to dissent in the matter of contraception. Neither can it be excluded a priori, he continues, that the Spirit is using that dissent to correct a teaching more quickly than would otherwise be possible.[63]

On the subject of divorce and remarriage another American theologian, Daniel Maguire, pointed out that the church went beyond Scripture in granting the Pauline privilege and thus deciding that indissolubility did not apply in that case.[64]

> In this instance divorce and remarriage were seen as a value even though without scriptural warranty. Clearly, then, the "deposit of faith," whatever riches it contains for morality, does not do the moralist's work.[65]

We shall see in later chapters that some of the theologians opposed to proportionalism argue that the powers of the magisterium are wider than those admitted by the proportionalists. First, however, we must see how proportionalism got off the ground. Here in this chapter we are considering how and why some theologians have been "converted" to this more teleological approach to moral norms. Why some others were not will, we hope, become clear when we examine their arguments in later chapters.

(d) *New Thought on the Specificity of Christian Ethics*   To many it may seem that there are grounds for thinking that a small number of behavioral norms exist only within certain restricted Christian circles. The ban on divorce and remarriage (except in certain circumstances) could help to create that impression, and so too could the ban on artificial contraception. The debate on the specificity of Christian ethics is therefore not totally unrelated to the discussion on the magisterium, and, like that discussion, has been of some importance for the acceptance and development of proportionalism in the United States.

During the period under discussion, a number of theologians were asking questions such as: Is there a specifically Christian ethics? Does the Christian faith add anything to the material content, to what we can know by reason in the field of ethics? The answer to such questions, as

McCormick later put it, "affects the Church's competence to teach morality authoritatively, and how this is to be achieved and implemented." If Christian faith did add some material content to what is knowable by reason, he says, this very fact could provide support for a very juridical notion of the moral magisterium. Our understanding of the natural law would also be affected, as could the very processes we use to determine the rightness or wrongness of many concrete projects.[66]

A number of moralists, while not denying that there was something specific to Christian morality, pointed out that the distinction was not to be found in the content of concrete moral norms based on what is authentically human.[67] Some of the most influential contributions came from the pen of Josef Fuchs, who pointed out that the specificity of Christian ethics is to be found in the believer's fundamental decision for God in Jesus Christ. He calls this fundamental decision and attitude "Christian intentionality." It is a "full, personal, enduring decision, a being decided in each particular situation."[68] What we are concerned with here is the realization of the person as person before the Absolute. Now, while we tend to reflect in a more or less thematic way about the particular categorical aspects of our lives, this self-realization before the Absolute cannot be the object of a full thematic reflection. This nonthematic awareness, however, far from being a lower form or degree of consciousness, is richer and deeper than the thematic reflexive type. Moreover, "the aspect of self-realization of the person before the Absolute constitutes objectively the more essential and decisive element of the moral act, in contrast to the aspect of the particular-categorical doing of justice, of one's duty to the family, etc."[69] But what about the categorical aspect? Is there anything specifically Christian in it?

> If we abstract from the decisive and essential element of Christian morality, of "Christian intentionality" as transcendent aspect, Christian morality, in its categorical orientation and materiality is basically and substantially a "Humanum," that is, a morality of genuine being human. This means that truthfulness, uprightness and faithfulness are not specifically Christian, but generally human values in what they materially say, and that we have reservations about lying and adultery, not because we are Christian, but simply because we are human.[70]

Such a clarifying of issues was and is of immense importance. If the specificity of Christian ethics is not to be found in its categorical aspects, what sense is there in claiming that certain acts (e.g., directly taking one's own life) are always illicit because God has not given permission for such acts (a point to which we shall need to return later)? And could there really be any sense in any claim that the official magisterium could have special insights enabling it to see that certain acts are illicit even though this cannot be demonstrated in a way acceptable to human reason?

(e) *New Thought on the Natural Law*   In 1966 Milhaven had this to say about what he called "natural law morality":

> As it stands, the principle is unexceptionable. Clearly, everything created should be used for the purpose God has marked for it. And God's purpose is its purpose. But when the principle is applied, e.g., to marriage, to the physical life of deformed babies, to sexual activity, to man's speech, its meaning loses clarity, even becomes ambiguous, at least in the eyes of the nonspecialist.[71]

But how, he goes on to ask, can we know the absolute and inviolable purpose of anything? Some values, he says, we recognize immediately upon discerning what they are. If, for example, we discern what can be the authentic love between a man and a woman, we recognize its absolute worth. "One need not consult the further consequences of the act."[72] However, the same immediate evidence cannot be found for all acts in which a moral decision is required. Even if a man understands what marriage is and what indissolubility would be, it does not seem to follow that he would, as a result of that, see clearly that marriage should always be contracted as indissoluble. Ethicians themselves, in fact, cite ulterior evidence in support of the indissolubility of marriage. "This is the final focus of the epistemological question: what is the nature of the 'further evidence'?"[73]

Milhaven suggests that this further evidence is, in the last analysis, always empirical. It is, he says, "the evidence of the probable or certain consequences, of what is going to result from the act in question."[74] The agent asks himself if the eventual result will contribute to or oppose the concrete realization of the absolute values he has already recognized (e.g., human love). Evidence of what will result can only be found in the evidence of past events, which indicate "what generally happens."[75]

It would probably be fair to say that a so-called "classical," unchanging view of the world was (and is?) to be found among those who based moral norms on "the purpose written in things." Bernard Lonergan tackled this problem in a short article published in 1967. He compared two positions to be found in the church. One, he said, may be called classicist, conservative or traditional, while the other may be called modern, liberal, or perhaps historicist. What is involved here are two different understandings of mankind. We can, he says, apprehend man in an abstract way through a definition that applies *omni et soli* and through properties which are verifiable in every man. In this way, we know man as such, an unchanging abstraction. Clearly, this view of things gives rise to no requirements for change in form, structure and method, because change takes place in the concrete and this view excludes the concrete. However, this exclusion of change in forms, structures and method is not theological. It is, says Lonergan, "grounded simply upon a certain conception of scientific or philosophical method." That conception, he adds, is no longer the only one or even the commonly conceived one. We can also apprehend mankind "as a concrete aggregate developing over time where the locus of development and, so to speak, the synthetic bond is the emergence, expansion, differentiation, dialectic of meaning and of meaningful performance." Meaning or intentionality is here "a constitutive component of human living," and this component is not fixed, static or unchangeable. It is instead "shifting, developing, going astray, capable of redemption." According to this way of looking at things, says Lonergan, we find in the historicity which results from human nature, a demand for changing forms, structures and methods. It is through this medium of changing meaning that divine revelation has come into the world, and it is through this medium that the church gives witness to it.[76]

This more dynamic view of things was shared by other scholars. Fuchs declared that the natural moral law cannot be regarded as a static quantity and reality which is preserved in books as a list of precepts and commands. Rather it must be understood as "the ever new and still to be solved problem of being a person of this world."[77] Development and progress are implied here. Moreover, while many branches of knowledge concerned with human behavior and conduct will not require repeated calling into question, other areas of knowledge touching on solutions to problems concerning rightness and goodness will be open to doubt.

> Most important of all, completely new questions are constantly arising, particularly at a time when man's probing into the facts of nature and their changing character make it possible for him, as a result of experience, to regard previous answers to questions, which may have been well-intentioned, as in fact basically "inhuman and therefore incorrect."[78]

Schüller pointed out that we must distinguish between the moral norms that are based on man's unchangeable metaphysical nature and those based on his changing historicity.

> The questionable restriction of natural law norms to those based on the unchangeable metaphysical nature of man seems to stem from a fear of relativism and an attempt to avoid its dangers by estimating what is historically changeable in man as narrowly as possible.[79]

However, the grounding of an ought in being does leave room for change since it merely states the correlation between them. The extent to which man remains unchanged throughout the process of historical change is not a problem for ethics. That, says, Schüller, is an area for metaphysical anthropology. However, "precisely to the extent that man's being changes with time must the applicable ethical norm also change in every case."[80]

A more personalistic approach to the subject of natural law also came into the writing of some moralists at this time. Fuchs, for example, said that what we call nature is matter to be formed by man, to be humanized and personalized by man. "For a truly human morality, moral action means nothing other than 'being human,' 'being rational'."[81] Further on in the same article he points out that, in physical nature as such, we can read directly only facts to which the physical laws of nature pertain. We thus see that it is a physical law that a rape may result in the victim's becoming pregnant and that such a consequence could be prevented by a premature suspension of ovulation. We cannot discern from physical nature as such, however, which use of the physical laws is morally justifiable. In order to discover what is morally right in the use of physical reality and physical laws, we need to understand "the meaning, the significance and the importance of the given physical nature in the totality of the human person as such." We cannot find norms for correct moral behavior in mere conformity to physical nature as such. What matters is conformity to the human person in his or her totality. "Thus it is not the physical law that has to be considered as a moral law and invoked to regulate the free actions of mankind, but the *'recta ratio'* which understands the *person* in the *totality* of his reality."[82]

Bernard Häring pointed out that man must not be dominated by biological and psychological processes if "he can modify these processes in the direction of greater moral freedom and a better interpersonal relationship."[83] Man, he goes on to say, is not only called to shape events, but also to transform natural processes "and even to administrate his own biological and psychological heritage."[84]

Before leaving aside the subject of natural law for the time being, it might be useful to add a few words about comments made regarding the writings of St. Thomas. Convinced that most present-day champions of natural law trace their origins to Aquinas, Milhaven produced a study on the subject of absolutes in the writings of the same. In this work he analyzes Thomas's treatment of a number of biblical incidents in which "God seemed to authorize a violation of the negative moral absolutes Thomas held."[85] He concludes that, although for Aquinas the act and its physical effects were relevant factors, the "moral center of gravity" was not to be found in them. The legitimacy of the means, provided the act contributed to a good purpose, depended upon the authority of the person acting. "Abortion and premarital sexual intercourse would be absolutely wrong if the agent had only normal human authority. But God could, by a special initiative, authorize a man to perform the same acts."[86]

So, says Milhaven, the point of division between the more relativistic ethics of the twentieth century and Thomas is not the question whether certain means are always wrong because of their physical effects. It is rather

> whether or not God has shared with man the authority and dominion to take certain means when, perhaps by way of exception, they serve the greater good. The question for dialogue, therefore, is how far God has shared his dominion with man.[87]

Notes

1. The terms "proportionalism" and "proportionalist" seem to have come into vogue in the United States after Richard McCormick's review of an article by John Connery in which the latter had described Peter Knauer, Bruno Schüller, Josef Fuchs and others as "tending towards consequentialism" (R.A. McCormick, *Notes on Moral Theology 1965 through 1980* (Lanham, Md., 1981), 537–43, esp. 541). Connery accepted McCormick's point that those authors were not consequentialists, and in a later article wrote: "This study will attempt initially to explain a new norm for making rules, commonly known as proportionalism" (J.R. Connery, "Catholic Ethics: Has the Norm for Rule-Making Changed?," *Theological Studies* 42 (1981): 232–50, here 232). Just how common it was is difficult to say, but McCormick records the use of the term by Donald McCarthy, William May and John Harvey in 1977 (*Notes . . . 1965 through 1980*, 697–98).

2. See B. Schüller, "What Ethical Principles Are Universally Valid?," *Theology Digest* 19 (1971): 23–28.

3. P. Knauer, "La détermination du bien et du mal moral par le principe du double effet," *Nouvelle Revue Théologique,* 87 (1965): 356–76.

4. Throughout this work, quotations, etc. from McCormick's "Notes" published earlier than 1986 will be taken from his two collections: *Notes on Moral Theology 1965 through 1980* (Washington, D.C., 1981) and *Notes on Moral Theology 1981 through 1984* (Lanham, Md., 1984).

5. For further discussion of this point, see: H.G. Kramer, *The Indirect Voluntary or Voluntarium in Causa* (Washington, D.C., 1935); V. Alonso, *El principio del doble efecto en los comentadores de Santo Tomaso de Aquino desde Cayetano hasta los Salmanticenses. Explicación del derecho de defensa según Santo Tomaso de Aquino* (Rome, 1937); J. Mangan, "An Historical Analysis of the Principle of Double Effect," *Theological Studies* 10 (1949): 41–61; J. Ghoos, "L'acte à double effet. Etude de théologie positive," *Ephemerides Theologicae Lovanienses* 27 (1951): 30–52. Not all of these authors agree that the principle of double effect can be traced back to St. Thomas. Ghoos, for instance, holds that it was the fruit of a theological evolution stretching from 1575 to 1630. John of St. Thomas was the first, he believes, to formulate the principle explicitly, around the year 1630 (see Ghoos, art. cit., 48). See also L. Rossi, "Il limite del principio del duplice effetto," *Rivista di Teologia Morale* 4 (1972): 11–37, esp. 17: "S. Tommaso, infatti, trattò del duplice effetto solo incidentalmente, per rispondere a difficoltà contro la legittima difesa (II.II,64,7). Nell'era moderna si è formulato e assolutizzato il principio (raggiungendo anche buone precisazioni)." For other comments on the historical background, see M. Attard, *Compromise in Morality* (Rome, 1976), 234, footnote 59, and L.I. Ugorji, *The Principle of Double Effect. A Critical Appraisal of Its Traditional Understanding and Its Modern Interpretation* (Frankfurt, 1985), 41–45.

6. P. Knauer, art. cit., 359.

7. Ibid., 357.

8. "Le sujet moral ne peut admettre un effet mauvais de son acte que si cet effet n'est qu'indirect, étant compensé par une raison proportionnée." Ibid.

9. Ibid.

10. "Quand la latière baratte, elle obtient nécessairement comme sous-produit du babeurre, même sans en avoir l'intention: tout en étant nécessaire, cet effet peut rester accidentel à l'intention de faire du beurre." Ibid., 359.

11. Ibid., 365.

12. Ibid., 366.

13. Ibid., 368.

14. R.A. McCormick, *Notes . . . 1965 through 1980,* 10.

15. Ibid., 10–11.

16. Ibid., 11.

17. D.F. O'Callaghan, "May a Spy Take His Life?," *Irish Ecclesiastical Record* 103 (1965): 259–64.

18. R.A. McCormick, *Notes . . . 1965 through 1980,* 32–33.

19. Ibid., 11.

20. P. Knauer, "The Hermeneutic Function of the Principle of Double Effect," *Readings in Moral Theology, No. 1: Moral Norms and Catholic Tradition,* ed. C.E. Curran and R.A. McCormick (New York, 1979), 38, footnote 12. See also P. Knauer, "La détermination. . . ," 360–61.

21. R.A. McCormick, *Notes. . . 1965 through 1980,* 312.

22. Ibid., v.

23. Cornelius J. van der Poel seems to have been influenced by Knauer's thought in writing his article, "The Principle of Double Effect," in *Absolutes in Moral Theology?*, ed. C.E. Curran (Washington, D.C., 1968), 186–210.

24. Cf. C.E. Curran, "Dialogue with the Future: Roman Catholic Theology in the United States Faces the Seventies," in *Catholic Moral Theology in Dispute* (Notre Dame, Ind. 1972), 245–53, esp. 245–46.

25. This was the commonly held view. However, we shall see in Chapter Five that not all scholars agree that the original formulators of the principle of double effect would have regarded it as applicable to such cases.

26. C.E. Curran, "Absolute Norms and Medical Ethics," in *Absolutes in Moral Theology?*, ed. C.E. Curran (Washington, D.C., 1968), 113.

27. A concrete example of what many would surely have called an absurd situation came from outside the United States. Bernard Häring picked it up from an article published in 1959. A gynecologist was called to perform an operation on a woman to remove a benign uterine tumor. On the womb were some varicose veins which bled profusely. To save her from bleeding to death he opened the womb and removed the fetus. The uterus thereupon contracted and the bleeding ceased. The doctor was happy that the woman's life had been saved and that it was still possible for her to bear children. A noted moralist told him, however, that what he had done was, in his opinion, objectively wrong. "I would have been allowed to remove the bleeding uterus with the fetus itself, he said, but was not permitted to interrupt the pregnancy, even though the purpose was to save the mother, whereas the other way would have been a lawful direct intervention (prima intentio) and action to save life, as in the case of a cancerous uterus." B. Häring, *Medical Ethics* (Slough, 1972), 108. He is quoting from: H. Kramann, "Umstrittene Heilsmethoden in Gynäkologie," *Arzt und Christ* 5 (1959): 202ff.

28. C.J. Van der Poel, art. cit., 195.

29. W. Van der Marck, *Love and Fertility* (London, 1965), 33–34 (English version of *Liefde en vruchtbaarheid*, 1964).

30. L. Bright, "Introduction" to W. Van der Marck, *Love and Fertility*, vii.

31. J.J. Noonan, *Contraception: A History of Its Treatment by the Catholic Theologians and Canonists* (Cambridge, Mass., 1965), 532–33.

32. L.G. Wrenn, "Marriage—Indissoluble or Fragile?," in *Divorce and Remarriage in the Catholic Church*, ed. L.G. Wrenn (New York, 1973), 144–45.

33. J.P. Jossua, "Moral Theology Forum: The Fidelity of Love and the Indissolubility of Christian Marriage," *The Clergy Review*, 56 (1971): 176–77. This article was briefly reviewed by McCormick. See *Notes. . . . 1965 through 1980*, 375–76.

34. Ibid., 177.

35. Ibid., 181.

36. Ibid., 179–180.

37. B. Peters, T. Beemer and C. Van der Poel, "Co-habitation in 'Marital State of Mind'," *The Homiletic and Pastoral Review* 66 (1966): 577.

38. C.E. Curran, "Divorce in the Light of a Revised Moral Theology," in *Ongoing Revision: Studies in Moral Theology* (Notre Dame, Ind., 1975), 105–06.

39. In view of the fact that the situation ethics of Robinson, Fletcher et al. was generally rejected by Catholic theologians, it has not been included in this section. However, there are grounds for thinking that situation ethics may have acted at least as a catalyst in some

of the processes going on in Catholic theological circles in the United States during the period under discussion. McCormick accused Fletcher of being ambiguous and of using flamboyant rhetoric as if it were moral reasoning (*Notes . . . 1965 through 1980*, 77, 586). However, in 1971 he admitted: "We have been forcefully reminded that traditional moral approaches, at least in the hands of their latter day practitioners have too easily underestimated the situational aspects, especially consequences, in decision-making." On the other hand, "this neglect has not been and will hardly be adequately corrected within a presentation so individualistic, and ultimately intellectually dissatisfying as that of Joseph Fletcher" (ibid., 295). Milhaven and Casey thought that there were some things in the "new morality" debate that seemed to call the Catholic tradition in question (J.G. Milhaven and D.J. Casey, "Introduction to the Theological Background of the New Morality," *Theological Studies* 28 (1967): 244). Although he had definite reservations about Fletcher's methodology, Curran was willing to admit that the other man's approach reflected a way of looking at reality which was "more suitable to modern man than the approach frequently employed in moral theology" (C.E. Curran, "Dialogue with Joseph Fletcher," in *A New Look at Christian Morality* (Notre Dame, Ind.: University of Notre Dame Press, 1968), 169).

40. W. Van der Marck, art. cit., 42.
41. Ibid.
42. Ibid., 44–53.
43. Ibid., 53.
44. Ibid., 57.
45. Ibid., 57–58.
46. Ibid., 58–59.
47. Ibid., 60.
48. P. Chirico, "Tension, Morality and Birth Control," *Theological Studies* 28 (1967): 285.
49. R.A. McCormick, *Notes . . . 1965 through 1980*, 123.
50. C.E. Curran, "Dialogue with Joseph Fletcher," 172.
51. R.A. McCormick, *Notes . . . 1965 through 1980*, 127.
52. D. Hurley, "A New Principle—When Right and Duty Clash," *The Furrow* 17 (1966): 621.
53. R.A. McCormick, *Notes . . . 1965 through 1980*, 125.
54. R.A. McCormick, "The New Morality," *America* 18 (1968): 771.
55. R.A. McCormick, "Past Church Teaching on Abortion," in *Proceedings of the Catholic Theological Society of America* 23 (1968), 150.
56. Regarding Küng's book *Unfehlbar? Eine Anfrage* (later translated into English as *Infallible? An Inquiry*), J.J. Hughes wrote: "The Italian translation, published even before the original for motives too obvious to require statement here, predictably caused the editor of *Osservatore Romano* to explode like a rocket streaking across the Roman heavens: two lengthy articles in the semi-official Vatican organ denounced the Swiss theologian and all his works, while failing to convey to readers even the barest summary of the book's contents." J.J. Hughes, "Infallible? An Inquiry Considered," *Theological Studies* 32 (1971): 183.
57. *AAS*, vol. 42, 568.
58. R.A. McCormick, "The Magisterium and Theologians," *Proceedings of the Catholic Theological Society of America* (1969), 241.

59. See R.A. McCormick, *Notes . . . 1965 through 1980,* 197–98, esp. his remarks about the writings of Gregory Baum.

60. John Cardinal Heenan, "The Authority of the Church," *The Tablet* 222 (1968): 488.

61. R.A. McCormick, *Notes . . . 1965 through 1980,* 199.

62. J.A. Komonchak, "Ordinary Papal Magisterium and Religious Assent," in *Readings in Moral Theology No. 3,* ed C.E. Curran and R.A. McCormick, 80–81. First published in *Contraception: Authority and Dissent,* ed. C.E. Curran (New York), 101–26.

63. Ibid.

64. D.C. Maguire, "Morality and Magisterium," in *Readings in Moral Theology No. 3,* 40. This article was first published in *Cross Currents* 18 (1968): 41–65. Maguire refers to Rudolf Schnackenburg's discussion of the Pauline privilege and Scripture in *The Moral Teaching of the New Testament* (New York, 1965), 249. See also T.J. Deidun, *New Covenant Morality in Paul* (Rome 1981). Deidun points out that in 1 Cor. 7:15, the verb χωρισθῆναι is not likely to mean "divorce." In v. 11 of the same chapter Paul clearly uses it to mean "separate," as the right to remarriage is expressly denied there. The expression οὐ δεδούλωται is not, moreover, "a declaration that the marriage bond has been dissolved." Elsewhere Paul uses δεδέσθαι when referring to the marriage bond, and it is unlikely, says Deidun, that he would associate marriage as such with the condition of enslavement. "What he is saying in v. 15 in effect is: 'if the non-christian partner goes, let him(her) go . . . ; in matters (situations) like this . . . the christian partner is not so dependent . . . on living with a spouse that he(she) has to lose his(her) peace by trying to prevent the inevitable. The overriding consideration is peace, the goal of the christian vocation' " (op. cit., 174).

65. Ibid., 40–41. The debate on the magisterium continued on throughout the 1970s and spilled over into the eighties. A number of later contributions (European and American) are included in the collection referred to above, edited by Curran and McCormick. Recent contributions are: F.A. Sullivan, *Magisterium. Teaching Authority in the Catholic Church* (New York, 1983); P. Chirico, *Infallibility. The Crossroads of Doctrine* (Wilmington, Del., 1983). See also Germain Grisez's reaction to Sullivan's book: "Infallibility and Specific Moral Norms: A Review Discussion," *The Thomist* 49 (1985): 248–87.

66. R.A. McCormick, *Notes . . . 1965 through 1980,* 627.

67. See, for example, C.E. Curran, "Is There a Distinctively Christian Social Ethic?," in *Metropolis: Christian Presence and Responsibility,* ed. P.D. Morris (Notre Dame, Ind., 1970).

68. J. Fuchs, "Is There a Specifically Christian Morality?," in *Readings in Moral Theology No. 2,* ed. C.E. Curran and R.A. McCormick (New York, 1980), 6. This article originally appeared in German under the title: "Gibt es eine spezifisch christliche Moral?," *Stimmen der Zeit* 185 (1970): 99–112, but was reviewed by McCormick along with Fuchs's "Human, Humanist and Christian Morality," in *Human Values and Christian Morality* (Dublin, 1970), 112–47. See R.A. McCormick, *Notes . . . 1965 through 1980,* 297–98.

69. Ibid., 7.

70. Ibid., 8. Like the debate on the magisterium, this debate on the specificity of Christian ethics also continued. Later contributions from both sides of the Atlantic are included in the collection referred to above, edited by Curran and McCormick.

71. J.G. Milhaven, "Towards an Epistemology of Ethics," *Theological Studies* 27 (1966): 228.

72. Ibid., 233.
73. Ibid.
74. Ibid., 235.
75. Ibid.
76. B. Lonergan, "The Transition from a Classicist World View to Historical Mind-edness," in *Law for Liberty: The Role of Law in the Church Today,* ed. J.E. Biecher (Baltimore: Helicon, 1967), 129–30.
77. J. Fuchs, "Moral Aspects of Human Progress," in *Theology Meets Progress,* ed. P. Land (Rome, 1971), 150–51. This was originally one of a series of lectures given at the Gregorian University, Rome in 1969.
78. Ibid., 151.
79. B. Schüller, "Can Moral Theology Ignore Natural Law?," *Theology Digest* 15 (1967): 97.
80. Ibid.
81. J. Fuchs, "Human, Humanist and Christian Morality," 116.
82. Ibid.
83. B. Häring, "Dynamism and Continuity in a Personalistic Approach to Natural Law," in *Norm and Context in Christian Ethics,* ed. G.H. Outka and P. Ramsey (London, 1969), 206.
84. Ibid.
85. J.G. Milhaven, "Moral Absolutes and Thomas Aquinas," in *Absolutes in Moral Theology?,* 181.
86. Ibid., 182.
87. Ibid., 183. Much later, John F. Dedek produced some interesting articles on similar themes: "Intrinsically Evil Acts: An Historical Study of the Mind of St. Thomas," *The Thomist* 43 (1979): 385–413, and "Moral Absolutes in the Predecessors of St. Thomas," *Theological Studies* 38 (1977): 654–80. In the latter work Dedek concludes that the theologians discussed were of the opinion that certain acts were bad in themselves. However, the fundamental reason they give for the unjustifiableness of these acts is not that the matter (*materia*) is bad. They can never be justified because the words used to describe them (fornication, stealing, etc.) "designate more than the act in *materia indebita;* they imply that they are done *ex libidine,* from selfish desire preferring a creature to God." However, God can "separate the material act from its bad end and give it a good end. Then he can order the action or dispense from its prohibition because it is no longer motivated by selfish interest but by a good end. But then the act is no longer properly described by the term which implies bad will" (art. cit., 679). This, of course, brings us back to the question posed by Milhaven: How far has God shared his dominion with man? An even more recent article by Dedek is: "Intrinsically Evil Act: The Emergence of a Doctrine," *Recherches de théologie ancienne et médiévale* 50 (1983): 191–226.

CHAPTER TWO

A New Beginning

Having read thus far and been influenced by what they have read, some readers might be tempted to conclude something like the following:

> If our moral rules are not absolutes but empirical generalisations, no specific action can be regarded as *malum in se* quite apart from its context and there is no ethical significance in the distinction, so basic to the manualist approach, between evil that is *directe voluntarium* or *indirecte voluntarium tantum*. Instead, one should be free to base moral decisions on the actual consequences of one's behavior as these are foreseen to occur. This may sound simple in theory. It is never simple in fact. In conflict situations it will be a matter of assessing all the moral good and all the moral evil implicated in each of the options available as feasible responses to one's situation and of electing and following out that alternative which appears most favorable to human welfare. Here the moral ambiguity of such a response needs to be fully recognised and any moral evil involved needs to be made the subject of Christian repentance.[1]

This, however, comes very close to the Lutheran way of thinking, something carefully avoided by the proportionalists. What they were and are concerned with is the right solution to a moral problem. If the solution is right, it cannot at the same time be wrong, and, if it is not wrong, why should the moral agent repent?[2]

It should be clear from the start that no proportionalist condones the production of moral evil. Unless that much is understood right at the beginning, what follows will be largely incomprehensible.

In the various changes that were taking place in the world of moral theology, Milhaven saw a general trend towards giving more importance to love and less to law in Christian moral decision making. He was glad, however, that the situation ethics debate was losing its fascination and hoped "to advance current discussion even further beyond the debate."[3] If love is simply that which "seeks the good of anybody, everybody,"[4] on what basis, he asks, do we evaluate the good in a situation? One widespread line of reply "identifies the good with 'whatever works', i.e., with helpful consequences."[5] A further step is to ask: granted that I know what some of the consequences of a certain decision are likely to be, how can I evaluate them? For illumination, Milhaven turns to the proportionate assessment of values and disvalues. However, he points out, the principles governing such assessment are fluid, often difficult to apply and resist verbal communication. We often talk about a hierarchy of values, but, although in most cases of conflict we would choose a certain value "x" over value "y," there are times when we would choose "y" in preference to "x."

To overcome the apparent impasse reached at this point, Milhaven resorts to what he calls a love epistemology. Contemporary ethics, he says, is in agreement with medieval moral theology that "affective or appetitive orientations of the individual make possible, directly or indirectly, moral insight, but would think of examples rather in terms of categories of present day psychology than in those of the classical virtues."[6] He takes up the example of a person in a position of authority (e.g., parent, teacher or religious superior) who has to decide whether or not to punish someone who is guilty of a dereliction. He or she must sift the facts of the case, see what the likely consequences are, and evaluate them. Obviously, says Milhaven, only the parent, the teacher, or the religious superior who habitually has "an open, loving, confident relationship to other persons" will be able to see what is best for the person in their charge and for their community in this particular situation.[7] In short, Milhaven sees experience as being central to contemporary ethics. Only experience (one's own and that of other people) generates the love that makes it possible for us to have insight into values and disvalues, and that insight itself takes place in experience, the value being known as experienced.[8]

Milhaven's approach, if we latch on to his own terminology, could perhaps be called "consequentialism for those who love rightly." As such, however, I would see it as something of a disappointment for people who have pondered the moral wrongs committed by morally good people: the preaching of the Second Crusade by St. Bernard; the burning of heretics by well-intentioned Christians; . . . etc. Enormous mistakes made by real lovers! Like Curran, Milhaven did well to highlight certain problems. He also did well in underlining the importance of experience, but again we see the need to come to grips with the distinction between the moral goodness or sinfulness of a person and the rightness or wrongness of his/her acts.

Interestingly, Milhaven makes no reference to Knauer in this article. And yet, a somewhat abridged English version of the latter's first article was published in the United States in 1967, and, in the same year, an English translation of a second article by the same author on the same subject appeared. In this second article, Knauer's basic thesis remained unchanged. That is: "One may permit the evil effect of his act only if this is not intended in itself but is indirect and justified by a commensurate reason."[9]

When speaking about what is intended, Knauer distinguishes between what he calls "psychological intention" and "moral intention." He explains this distinction by saying that the moral agent may intend an injury in the moral sense even if he or she would prefer its absence or is not even thinking much about it. The converse, he says, is also true. That is, an effect can be beyond moral intention even if the person acting is psychologically concentrated on that very effect.[10]

When we speak about our motive or reason for acting, we sometimes use the word "end," and, says Knauer, we could substitute the term "intention." While, however, keeping clear in our minds this particular meaning of these terms, we must consider another concept which, in ethics, is also called "intention." The motive or reason, says Knauer, is not in itself an ethical concept. The motive a person has for acting is always good (in the premoral sense). From that alone, therefore, we can learn nothing about the rightness or wrongness of the act. Hence the need for this second concept which gives a wider meaning to the word "intention": the reason for an act "no longer considered *alone* but in its relation to the act itself."[11] In other words, what is intended in the moral sense can be described as "the reason of the act insofar as it is in correspondence with the totality of the act or not."[12] This meaning of "intention" corresponds, says Knauer, to St. Thomas's use of the term *finis operis*. For the sake of clarity and to help us understand better what Knauer has to say on this point, it might be useful to quote Thomas as he does:

> I reply that it must be said that nothing prevents there being two effects of one act, of which one effect alone would be in the intention and the other would be beyond intention. But moral acts receive their species according to what is intended, not from what is beyond intention, since the latter is accidental as appears from what has been said above.
>
> Therefore, from the act of someone defending himself a double effect can follow: one is the preservation of his own life, the other is the killing of

the attacker. An act of this kind in which the preservation of one's own life is intended does not have the character of the unlawful, since it is natural for everyone to preserve himself in his being as far as he can.

But some act arising from a good intention can be made unlawful if it is not proportionate to the end. And so, if someone in defending his own life uses greater violence than is necessary, it will be unlawful. But if he moderately repels violence, it will be lawful defence.[13]

Now, according to what Thomas writes elsewhere, notes Knauer, moral acts are determined by the *finis operis* (the end of the act). Here Thomas says that they are determined by "what is intended." Although it may seem surprising at first glance to say that what St. Thomas must mean is not the *finis operantis* (the end of the person acting) but the *finis operis*, we see that, unless we are prepared to admit contradiction with the passages elsewhere, the *finis operis* must mean "what is intended."[14]

The problem is solved, he says, by understanding *finis operis* to mean not just the external effect, but "the act which is willed and intended as such."[15] In the case of almsgiving, therefore, what the action is (bribe, repayment of a loan, a present, etc.) depends on what the donor wills the action objectively to be. What matters is not the donor's "arbitrary declaration" but his or her actual intent. Any unjustified evil which comes about in the pursuit of a value is morally intended and belongs to the *finis operis*.[16]

Knauer goes on to explain that the *finis operantis* is the act to which the agent relates his or her first act. For example, somebody may give alms in order to gain a tax benefit. In such a case the *finis operantis* of the first act is identical to the *finis operis* of the second act. If an act is performed without being related to a second act, there is, strictly speaking, no *finis operantis*.[17]

If, then, the reason or motive is commensurate with the totality of the act, it constitutes the *finis operis* (the intention in the moral sense). In that case, any concomitant evil is not part of the *finis operis;* in other words, it is beyond or outside the agent's intention (*praeter intentionem*). If, however, there is a contradiction between the reason for the act and the act itself, then that reason does not constitute the *finis operis* of that act. The *finis operis* is instead composed of the evil effect of the act.

It is at this point that the terms "direct" and "indirect" become important. A common interpretation of the principle of double effect has been that, if the evil effect physically precedes the good that is willed and is therefore the means to its achievement, that evil is directly willed, and the whole act is thus rendered evil because a good end does not justify evil means. However, points out Knauer, if we say that this particular good end does not justify a certain means, we are presupposing that the means is already recognized as *morally* evil. But it is only after we have applied the principle of double effect that we can say whether or not we are dealing with moral evil. The mere fact that physical evil is involved in the means does not mean that the means is morally evil.

As in the case of the term "intention," Knauer speaks of a moral sense for the word "direct":

> Clearly there are cases in which the causing or permitting of an evil precedes the achievement of the end without the act thereby becoming morally bad. The evil is justified by a commensurate reason; although the cause is physically direct, it is not direct in a moral sense . . . The act is morally bad if the evil is direct or formal, that is, if the act is willed in such a way that there is no commensurate reason for it.[18]

It would seem, therefore, that, for Knauer, to say that the evil is direct (in the moral sense) is the same as to say that it is intended (in the moral sense). Similarly, if the evil is outside the intention in the moral sense, it is indirect in the moral sense. In the case of an ectopic pregnancy, therefore, the problem of removing the fetus is resolved. The saving of the mother is not a *direct* killing in the moral sense. However, "without a commensurate reason an evil is always willed directly, even if attention is not expressly directed to the evil but it is desired that there be no such evil."[19]

Knauer, it will be noted, had something to add to Milhaven's rather vague love epistemology. There is a way of measuring proportion, he says, even though quantitative comparison of qualitatively different values is impossible. If, in the last analysis, there is a contradiction between the act and the reason, the reason is not a commensurate one.[20] In other words, an act is morally wrong if "it is contradictory to the fullest achievement of its own end in relation to the whole of reality." In the short run, there is what Knauer calls "a 'more' of the value," but the price of this is "a 'lesser' achievement of the same value in the long run."[21]

Like Knauer (and Milhaven too in his earlier article on moral absolutes), Louis Janssens displayed more than a little interest in the writings of St. Thomas in his first major contribution to the debate. In this article Janssens stresses the role of intention. For Aquinas, he says, the *intentio* "is the striving towards the *end* to the extent that it is within the range of the *means*."[22] The intention, he goes on to say,

. . . is to will the end as a *reason* that the action is willed. When the end is bad, the whole action is the fruit of a *mala voluntas* and, because the action is only human as far as it emanates from the will (*voluntarius*), it is entirely bad.[23]

Then he goes on to illustrate this by citing St. Thomas's example of almsgiving when vanity motivates the giver. Here he describes love of vain praise as the intention, "that is, the cause and the reason (*ratio et causa*) of the action." The *finis operis* (providing relief) would be morally good if it were intended as end by the agent, but, in this case, the bad *intentio* of the agent is the reason.[24]

Still following Thomas, Janssens describes the human act as a composite unity, the interior act of the will being its formal element and the exterior act its material element. In other words, the formal element of a human act, he says, is the end (the proper object of the inner act of the will), while the material element of the same act is the means.[25]

Further on he states that, in Thomas's view, the good which is the object of the will is also its end. That good is a moral good if it corresponds to reason. It is, of course, still a good even if it does not correspond to reason, inasmuch as it is consonant with a particular appetite, but it is morally vitiated. Whether or not the moral good is the end of the subject's action depends on his or her inner disposition. "So the first moral qualification does not concern the particular acts but the subject himself, who by virtue of his virtuous dispositions is turned towards the moral good as his end."[26] The exterior action, according to Janssens' understanding of St. Thomas, becomes a concrete human act only insofar as it is directed toward an end which is within the inner disposition of the will of the person acting. "It is the end of the inner act of the will which specifies the malice or the goodness of the act."[27]

The moral goodness of the end, he says, is the formal element of the exterior act. So the goodness or badness of a human act gets its moral specification from the end. Now, the material element of this act gets its material specification from the object of the exterior action, but it is not just any kind of exterior action that can become the material element of a morally good end.[28] The exterior action is the means to the end. On account of its very definition as such, it must be proportionate to that end. Indeed, "the exterior act can only be means insofar as it is in proportion to the end."[29] So, in order to make a moral evaluation, says Janssens, we must first ask whether or not the end of the agent is morally good, and then ask if the exterior action is in due proportion to this end.[30]

We have seen that Knauer distinguishes between physical evil and moral evil. Janssens does the same thing, but prefers the term "ontic evil" to "physical evil" because the contemporary meaning of "physical" corresponds more to "material." Ontic evil is what we call "any lack of a perfection at which we aim, any lack of fulfilment which frustrates our natural urges and makes us suffer."[31] All our concrete actions involve ontic evils. This is unavoidable given our temporal and spatial limitations, our living together with others in the same material world, and our common sin-filled situation. No person can realize all the values open to him. He must make a choice, and in that very choosing there is a negation of value(s).[32] Concrete material norms aim at the elimination of ontic evil, but they cannot oblige us to do what is not possible. We should keep ontic evil to a minimum, but we cannot completely eliminate it in all its forms. Any attempt to do so, says Janssens, would make the actuation of our moral objectives impossible.[33] Having said all that, however, the fact remains that "we never have the right to will ontic evil as the *ultimate end of our intention,* because the formal element of our action, viz., the end, the object of the inner act of the will, would be morally evil, and the malice of the end determines and characterises the grade of morality of the entire action."[34] And, of course, even if the act has a good end, it is morally wrong if the means is not in due proportion to that end. It is obvious from what has been said so far that Janssens is not saying that the mere presence of ontic evil in the means is enough to make the act morally wrong. What he is saying is that, "when the single and composite act is viewed from the point of view of reason. . . , it must be found without an intrinsic contradiction between the *means* . . . and the morally good *end* of the inner act of the will."[35]

In this Janssens is, of course, in agreement with Knauer, and says so explicitly.[36] There are, however, differences of approach. Both men rely heavily on St. Thomas. In doing so, however, Janssens does not make far-reaching claims about the principle of double effect. Knauer, on the other hand, sees Aquinas's comments on self-defense as the first formulation of that principle, and keeps his exposition of Thomas' thought within its framework. One noteworthy result of this difference in approach would appear to be Janssens' lack of insistence upon the direct/indirect terminology that is so important to Knauer. His principle aim in this article is not, in fact, to show that any one principle is universal or fundamental, but rather "to explain the meaning and the significance of the *concrete material norms* of morality."[37] These norms, he says, prohibit ontic evil. They aim at an ideal, but, "insofar as they are *norms,* they imply only the obligation to realise that which is possible for man."[38] We must keep ontic evil to a minimum, and that we do, it would seem, by observing a basic principle, that Janssens shares with Knauer: i.e., there must be no contradiction between means and end. However, as we shall see later, Janssens adopted a somewhat different approach to the calculation of proportion in a later article, after having studied the writings of other authors.

Knauer, in effect, abandoned the first condition of the principle of double effect. Janssens' way of arguing would, moreover, appear to point in the same direction, so that he too would be forced to abandon it. That condition implies the conviction that certain actions are intrinsically evil, apparently meaning that the performance of any such action would always be morally wrong. That is the stand taken in the traditional manuals. The act of masturbation, for example, would never be permitted because, according to the manuals, such an act could never be merely a physical (ontic) evil.[39] If, however, we say that masturbation in its materiality alone is only an ontic evil, and that the same can be said for telling an untruth, killing oneself, artificial contraception, and all the other activities that, at one time or another, have been described as intrinsically evil, we come to a very important question: are there any absolute norms of behavior?

In 1966, John Coventry wrote that, in order to arrive at a "truly universal moral principle by moral judgment working inductively," we should need to enumerate all possible instances. If it were possible, for example, to see that all possible instances of extramarital intercourse would be wrong, then we could state, as a universal principle, that this whole class of actions was wrong. However, he asks, how can we know if and when we have considered all possible instances and situations?[40]

A few years later, in one of a series of lectures on the theology of human progress delivered at the Gregorian University in Rome, Fuchs declared that, although general moral principles which make a priori assertions about man's conduct as such are of considerable importance, alone they do not give us concrete guidelines for human behavior. "More concrete guidelines presuppose experience and knowledge of concrete reality and its possible method of realisation together with the consequences." He went on to ask if, in some areas of human action and behavior, it was possible to have several solutions, all of which were truly human and right. Where different cultures were concerned, he wondered if it was conceivable that slightly differing norms of behavior might, and even ought to, develop as a result of different contexts and partially different scales of values.[41]

Pursuing this line of thinking in an article which appeared a year or two later and was his first major contribution to the debate we are discussing, Fuchs declared that, at least on the theoretical level, "one cannot easily formulate universal norms of behavior in the strict sense of *intrinsece malum*."[42] In order to arrive at a behavioral norm, he says, we must take into account a whole complex of factors.

> What must be determined is the significance of the action as value or non-value for the individual, for interpersonal relations and for human society, in connection, of course, with the total reality of man and his society and in view of his whole culture. Furthermore, the priorities and urgency of the different values implied must be weighed. By this procedure, man as assessor (the evaluating human society) arrives at a judgment, tentatively or with some measure of certitude, as to which mode of behavior might further man's self-realization and self-development.[43]

Fuchs is careful to distinguish moral good/evil from premoral good/evil in this process. A human action or a person is morally good when the person "intends and effects a human good (value), in the premoral sense."[44] If the action involves premoral evil, this evil "must not be intended as such, and must be justified in terms of the totality of the action by appropriate reasons."[45] If the premoral evil is not justified by appropriate reasons, it is taken up into the agent's intention.

We cannot, therefore, have absolute moral norms (in the sense of concrete norms of human behavior)[46] unless circumstances and intention are taken into account. "The absoluteness of a norm depends more upon the objectivity of its relationship to reality than upon its universality."[47] Thus we can say that "every action that is objectively—*secundum rectam rationem*—not justified in the concrete human situation . . . is *intrinsece malum* and therefore absolutely to be avoided."[48]

A major point being made, then, by Fuchs in this article is that we cannot make moral judgments without knowing all the relevant circumstances and the intention of the agent. The means alone does not constitute the whole action. The act of placing the blade of a knife in a certain part of a person's body can be a curative measure, murder, self-defense, etc. It is impossible for us to foresee all the possible circumstances and intentions that could accompany any one particular action. That is enough to prevent the formulation of absolute behavioral norms on the theoretical level. It is, however, worth mentioning that Fuchs does not deny that, on the practical level, "there can be norms stated as universals, with precise delineations of action to which we cannot conceive of any kind of exception—e.g., cruel treatment of a child which is of no benefit to the child."[49]

Fuchs's approach to the problem of moral decision making in this article is very similar to Knauer's. When, he asks, is human action, or man in his action morally good? The answer, he suggests, is when he intends a human good, like joy or health, for example, in the premoral sense. The action is not morally good when he intends and effects a human nongood, in the premoral sense (as, for example, death or wounding). If his intending and effecting of a premoral good involve effecting evil, only good is intended "if the realization of the evil through the intended realization of good is justified as a proportionately related cause."[50]

This way of thinking, however, also builds on Fuchs's own personalistic approach to the subject of natural law, which we have already touched upon. Here he writes that traditionally the *lex naturalis* is stated to be a *lex interna,* not a *lex externa.* By *lex interna* he means man's possibility and duty of discerning what, in the concrete, human action is capable of being here and now, and what can be affirmed propositionally about behavioral norms. "Here we are obviously dealing with moral perceptions of an absolute nature, but it is equally obvious that absolute means, at least primarily, correspondence of behavior to personal human reality; objectivity, therefore, and not, or at least not primarily, universal validity."[51]

Fuchs had also been influenced by another German author, Bruno Schüller,[52] whose approach to the problems we have been discussing was somewhat less complicated than that of Knauer. With regard to universally binding norms, Schüller pointed out that some of them are mere tautologies. An example would be: "Do not kill unjustly." Others at least have the merit of really saying something, for example, "You must always love and hope in God." However, in among these so-called universal or absolute norms we find synthetic precepts, such as: "Every use of artificial means to impede conception is immoral." Although this last type is the more practical, it is also the most questionable. What do we do when there is a clash of values? Schüller's hypothesis is worded simply but carefully:

> Any ethical norm whatsoever regarding our dealings and omissions in relation to other men or the environment can be only a particular application of that more universal norm, 'The greater good is to be preferred'. The only unconditionally and unexceptionally obligatory norm is one which concerns a good than which no better can ever be conceived to exist. Be it noted that in this category we must at once include this special case: we can never do any good however great for a man by bringing him to act against his own conscience.[53]

In much of what he wrote over the next few years Schüller was influenced by what he found in British philosophy. We shall, however, have ample opportunity to discuss that, as well as other points raised in the writings of the proportionalists so far discussed, in the chapters that follow this one.

Conclusions to Be Drawn

It is difficult to say when proportionalism really took root in the United States. Little of importance was written by American authors in the early years of the debate. In the mid and late seventies, however, a number of theologians and philosophers in the United States wrote on the subject, some in favor of it and some most decidedly against it, these latter causing development in the debate through their opposition. There was certainly a climate of change in the United States, as elsewhere, in the period immediately following the Second Vatican Council. The development of thought in the various areas we discussed in the first chapter undoubtedly played some part in preparing the ground for the planting of proportionalism in North American soil, as did the glaring moral problems which we also mentioned.

Certainly, one of the most important factors was the entrance of McCormick into the proportionalist camp. In reviewing these last mentioned four articles by Knauer, Janssens, Fuchs and Schüller, McCormick was very favorable indeed.[54] He too was undoubtedly influenced by the various movements in thought and, as we have already had occasion to note, he admits to having been led by fellow theologians to change his opinion on certain issues. Evidently, some of his colleagues helped him to move from his "anti-Knauer" position to that of the principal champion of proportionalism in the English-speaking world.

Interestingly, W.B. Smith refers to a pre-*Humanae Vitae* McCormick and a post-*Humanae Vitae* McCormick.[55] The more noticeable changes in McCormick's thought do seem to have come about after the publication of the encyclical. Moreover, it is perhaps true that, even more than the situation ethics debate, *Humanae Vitae* acted as a catalyst to those who were seeking solutions to the moral problem most under discussion. Many who had expected a solution to the dilemma facing a large number of married couples were no doubt disillusioned when the encyclical appeared, and perhaps this, above all else, made a number of American theologians more disposed to listen to the theories of some of their European colleagues.

In the edition of his "Notes" in which he reviewed Schüller's article, Knauer's second contribution and an article written in a similar vein by Charles Robert,[56] McCormick wrote that all concluded that the causing of physical evil becomes immoral when it occurs without a proportionate reason and that the physically direct doing of evil is not decisive. There was, however, a slow development in this debate over the next decade or so and, as it proceeded, the points noted by McCormick became more nuanced. Three important distinctions dominated the debate and continue to do so. They are: the Moral Rightness/Moral Goodness Distinction; the Teleology/Deontology Distinction; and the Direct/Indirect Distinction. Each of the next three chapters will be devoted to one of these distinctions.

Notes

1. N. Crotty, "Conscience and Conflict," *Theological Studies* 32 (1971): 231.
2. See McCormick's review of this article by Crotty in his *Notes . . . 1965 through 1980,* 360–67.
3. J.G. Milhaven, "Objective Moral Evaluation of Consequences," *Theological Studies* 32 (1971): 408.
4. Ibid., 409. Here he is quoting Joseph Fletcher, *Situation Ethics* (Philadelphia, 1966), 107.
5. Ibid., 410.
6. Ibid., 423.
7. Ibid.
8. Ibid., 428.
9. P. Knauer, "The Hermeneutic Function of the Principle of Double Effect," 5.
10. Ibid., 4.
11. Ibid., 15 (emphasis mine).
12. Ibid.
13. Ibid., 3 (he is quoting from *Summa Theologiae,* II–II, q.64, a.7. *in corp.*).
14. Ibid., 4.
15. Ibid.
16. Ibid., 4–5.
17. Ibid., 5.
18. Ibid., 19–20.
19. Ibid., 21.
20. Ibid., 14.
21. Ibid.
22. L. Janssens, "Ontic Evil and Moral Evil," in *Readings . . . No. 1,* 45. This article was first published in *Louvain Studies* in 1972. It is difficult to ascertain how much immediate impact it had in the United States. McCormick did not review it until 1975.

Presumably, it escaped his attention until then. However, we find the article often referred to in works published after that date.

23. Ibid., 50.
24. Ibid., 50–51.
25. Ibid., 46–47.
26. Ibid., 47–48.
27. Ibid., 49.
28. Ibid., 52.
29. Ibid., 53.
30. Ibid., 78.
31. Ibid., 60.
32. Ibid., 60–66.
33. Ibid., 84–86.
34. Ibid., 70.
35. Ibid., 71.
36. Ibid., 72.
37. Ibid., 84.
38. Ibid., 86.

39. See, for example, J. Mausbach-G. Ermecke, *Katholische Moraltheologie, Vol. III,* (Münster Westfalen, 1961), 351–53.

40. J. Coventry, "Christian Conscience," *The Heythrop Journal* 7 (1966): 152.

41. J. Fuchs, "Moral Aspects of Human Progress," in *Theology Meets Progress,* ed. P. Land (Rome, 1971), 154. The lecture was delivered in January, 1969.

42. J. Fuchs, "The Absoluteness of Behavioral Moral Norms," in *Personal Responsibility and Christian Morality* (Washington, D.C., and Dublin, 1983), 141.

43. Ibid., 131.

44. Ibid., 136.

45. Ibid., 137. Fuchs was already thinking along similar lines a few years earlier. In a recently published article, Robert Blair Kaiser reports that in the spring of 1966, during one of the final group of meetings of a papal commission appointed to examine the issue of birth control, the then archbishop of Westminster, Cardinal Heenan, asked if it was possible to say that contraception is intrinsically evil, but permitted for sufficient reasons. "Fuchs, perhaps the most highly regarded moral theologian in the room, replied. 'If contraception were intrinsically evil, it could never be licit. All methods of contraception contain some evil, biological, psychological, et cetera, even periodic or continued abstinence. But this evil is permitted if some proportionate good demands it.' He added: 'In a case where a couple may use rhythm, they may also use other contraceptive means, if, for example, rhythm is hard to apply.' Heenan asked, 'What means?' Fuchs said, 'That would be determined by the couple, depending on their circumstances.' " R.B. Kaiser, "The Long Road to Birth Control Control," *National Catholic Reporter,* vol. 21, no. 27 (3 May 1985), 11. This article is a summary of a section of a book written by the same author and recently published by the Leaven Press. It is entitled: *The Politics of Sex and Religion.*

46. Fuchs does not deny the existence of *formal* norms which are absolute, but "the imperative to be just, chaste, and merciful . . . materially states nothing about the materially determined actions which can express justice, chastity and mercy" (ibid., 143). In fact, no proportionalist, to my knowledge, has ever put in doubt the existence of absolute formal norms. The whole discussion concerns only norms of behavior.

47. Ibid., 138.

48. Ibid., 142.

49. Ibid., 142.

50. Ibid., 136.

51. Ibid., 127–28.

52. In his later writings, as we shall see, Fuchs's approach is much closer to Schüller's than it is to Knauer's.

53. B. Schüller, "What Ethical Principles Are Universally Valid?," *Theology Digest* 19 (1971): 24.

54. That does not mean, as we shall see later, that he did not have reservations on some points.

55. W.B. Smith, "The Revision of Moral Theology in Richard A. McCormick," *Homiletic and Pastoral Review* 81 (1981): 9.

56. C. Robert, "La situation de 'conflit', un thème dangereux de la théologie morale d'aujourd'hui," *Revue des Sciences Religeuses* 44 (1970): 190–213.

CHAPTER THREE

The Moral Goodness / Moral Rightness Distinction

Long before the advent of the current debate on proportionalism, it was usual in Catholic moral theology circles to distinguish between "material sin" and "formal sin." To people not trained in scholastic philosophy, these terms could be somewhat confusing. It is, of course, highly unlikely that many people would be so misled as to think that material sins were made up of atoms and molecules while formal sins were committed by gentlemen in dinner jackets and ladies in long dresses. However, in view of the fact that already fifteen years or so ago Robert Dailey was saying that such scholastic language was "going out of fashion," a short explanation might not be out of place here.

According to St. Thomas, says Dailey, the substance of the human act is words, deeds, thoughts and desires. In the case of sin, these are its matter. The form of the sin, on the other hand, is the moral disorder of the act. It is the imprint of the agent's will, which chooses to love something that it should not love. It thus takes badness into itself, and becomes bad to that extent. "For the will is conformed to whatever it loves."[1] If, then, we study sin only from the point of view of the matter, continues Dailey, excluding the subjective point of view, we come to the distinction between material sin and formal sin.[2]

> *Material* sin, therefore, is a deviation from the objective order of things, considered solely from an external point of view. *Formal* sin is an act which I know or think is a deviation and freely will to do.[3]

The use of the word "sin" here is interesting. F.J. O'Connell writes that, for an act to be a sin, three conditions must be fulfilled. The first is that there must be some "moral deordination or defect in the act." At least, the agent must conceive it that way. The second is that "there must be some advertence of the intellect," while the third is that "there must be some consent of the will." O'Connell then adds in parentheses: "we are speaking of advertence and consent with reference to the *sinfulness* of the act, not merely to its *physical* entity."[4] This kind of language is, however, somewhat confusing. A little further on, O'Connell writes:

> A sin is material when a person does something objectively wrong without adverting to its sinfulness . . . A sin is *formal* when advertence and consent are present. It is possible to commit a formal sin which is not objectively a sin.[5]

But surely, if "adverting" is necessary for sin, material sin is not sin at all. So why call it sin? Examples of the kind of mistake that can (and did) arise from such confusing use of language abound. Many readers will remember having been told by pastors and teachers that masturbation is always a mortal sin. They will also have encountered people who have gone on desperate searches for a priest to whom they could confess the fact that they had committed the "mortal sin" of having missed Mass on Sunday through no fault of their own. Clearly, less confusing terminology was desirable.

1. Moral Rightness and Moral Goodness in the Early Contributions to the Debate

However, in spite of this state of affairs and the apparent decreasing popularity of scholastic language, the proportionalists made little or no attempt to replace it in their earliest contributions to the debate. Knauer, it will be remembered, held that "an act becomes immoral when it is contradictory to the fullest achievement of its own end in relation to the whole of reality."[6] He also said, "Moral evil, I contend, consists in the last analysis in the permission or causing of a physical evil which is not justified by a commensurate reason."[7] But what does he mean by "immoral"? And what does he mean by "moral evil"? Does he mean sin? And, if he does indeed mean sin, what kind of sin: material sin or formal sin? One might be tempted to say that it all depends upon the circumstances: If I know that there is no commensurate reason, I commit a formal sin; if, however, through no fault of my own, I do not know any such thing, then the sin is merely material. One might be tempted to say that, but Knauer himself writes: "A lie consists in telling what is false without a commensurate reason and therefore directly or *formally* causes the error of another."[8]

That this is not merely a slip of the pen, and that Knauer is therefore exclusively concerned with formal sin (real sin) is clear from his discussion about the *finis operis* and the *finis operantis*. To illustrate what he had to say, he chose, we have seen, St. Thomas's example of almsgiving. The person who, in giving alms, is seeking only vainglory, has that vainglory as *finis operantis*. His or her act is therefore sinful. The *finis operis* is the relief of hunger, or whatever. Knauer, however, says that the act of almsgiving to relieve suffering is aimed at vainglory. Thus vainglory is the *finis operis* of the full act of the giver in its totality. He is apparently not interested in judging whether or not the act without the addition of the *finis operantis* is right or wrong. In other words, Knauer does not seem to answer, or even ask, the question: "Is it right or wrong to give money to that poor old beggar outside St. Mary's Church who hasn't eaten for a week?" Some might be inclined to protest that he has asked the question, and that his answer is: "It is wrong if you do it to gain vainglory." If that is the case, however, is it right not to give the beggar anything at all, and let him die of hunger in such circumstances? Knauer does not deal with such problems because he is only interested in whether or not an act is a (formal) sin. In other words, he restricts his discussion to the subject of the moral goodness or badness of the person acting.

Janssens too retained the scholastic terminology in his first contribution. As a general principle, he writes, we can say that any action which involves ontic evil "becomes the material element of an immoral act if this ontic evil is *per se* the end of the intention." This is so because the end of the acting subject is an immoral one, and, as a formal element, this immoral end contaminates the totality of the action with its malice.[9]

Further on in the same article he writes that, to make a moral evaluation, we need to ask whether the end, the object of the inner act of the agent's will, is morally good and whether the exterior act has a *debita proportio* to that end or contains the negation of the very value or principle affirmed in the end.[10]

If the exterior action does contain the negation of the value or principle affirmed in the end, writes Janssens, there is no longer a morally good end. For example, when excessive violence is used in defending oneself, that excess is not a means to the end of self-defense. It is not sanctioned by the end as reason or cause. The excessive use of violence is thus implied in the intention as something willed for its own sake.[11]

In a footnote, Janssens does seem to consider the possibility of a merely material sin on the part of the agent resulting from inculpable ignorance or error and not from an evil inner disposition. However,

> We said that mental defects and spiritual deficiencies, such as ignorance and error, can be listed as ontic evil. We can leave them out of the study of our *human* acts, since acts are not *human* when ignorance, error, mental disturbances, etc. are the *cause* of the behaviour. Thomas would say that they keep an act from being *actus voluntarius*—an act which emanates from the will—and a human act.[12]

That is all very well, but one would have hoped that proportionalism was going to help us not to make so many errors. One would have thought that such was the aim of all this talk of calculating proportion. After all, we do not need to be told by theologians that doing what we know to be wrong is a sin. Many people are trying to do what is right and avoid doing what is wrong. Unfortunately, people make mistakes sometimes in working out what is right and what is wrong, and it is in that area that they would appreciate some help from the theologians and philosophers.

Fuchs, we have seen, said that human action or man in his action is morally good when he intends and effects a premoral good, but not when he intends and effects a premoral evil. He, like Knauer and Janssens, holds that a proportionate reason justifies the realization of premoral evil through the intended realization of premoral good.[13]

> The surgical operation is morally right, because the person acting desires and effects only a good—in the premoral sense—namely, restoration of health. If the surgeon were to do more than was required in performing this operation, that "more" would not be justified by the treatment indicated—that is, it would be taken up as an evil (in the premoral sense) into the surgeon's intention; it would be morally bad.[14]

Fuchs too seems to be concerned with moral goodness and (formal) sin. This is made more apparent in a reference he makes to killing. Killing because of avarice, he writes, cannot be morally good, while killing in self-defense may be.[15]

A moral judgment should only be made on a simultaneous consideration of the action, the circumstances, and the agent's purpose. The reason for this, writes Fuchs, is the fact that those three elements are not a combination of three human actions. They are a single human action. He returns to the example of a surgical operation. It is one healing action, not three (wounding, healing, with the purpose of restoring health).[16] That is true, but, as we have seen, Fuchs also says that the operation is morally right because the person acting desires and effects only a good. It is conceivable that the surgeon could have an ulterior motive for performing the operation. We do not know where his desiring and effecting terminate. In order to make a judgment on the so-called formal level, we would need to know precisely that. Does, however, the moral rightness of the act depend on that? We shall return to this point a little later. For the moment, suffice it to say that some important changes came into the writings of both Fuchs and Janssens later on as a result of insights provided by Schüller.

However, with regard to our present topic of discussion, Schüller's first article on proportionalism does not seem to have presented a very different approach from that of his colleagues. In that article, it will be recalled, he proposed the hypothesis that any ethical norm regarding our dealings and omissions in relation to other people or the environment can only be an application of the more universal norm, the greater good is to be preferred. There is, however, just a slight hint of that distinction which would be so important in his later writings and in those of some of his colleagues. In the German original he pointed out that the above-mentioned hypothesis covers only concrete behavioral norms, absolute, unconditional norms being necessary to cover matters of salvation and moral goodness. This distinction comes in a discussion about making a person act against his or her conscience. The shortened English language version states that one may never do any good however great for a man by making him act against his conscience, but does not state that this is so because acting in accordance with or against one's conscience is always on the plane of moral goodness or sinfulness (in the real, formal sense), whereas concrete behavioral norms are not.[17] However, we cannot really say that Schüller spelled out here the distinction between the level of moral goodness (or sinfulness) and that of the moral rightness (or wrongness) of the act in anything like the way he did in later works.

2. Moral Rightness and Goodness in Later European Works

The importance of the distinction between moral rightness and moral goodness on the one hand, and between moral wrongness and moral badness on the other, seems to have struck Schüller as a result of his study of British ethical philosophy. We too, therefore, shall make a short excursion into that same area. Writing many years before the start of the proportionalist debate, G.E. Moore pointed out that what is deserving of moral praise or blame is often confused with the question as to what is right or wrong.

> I do not mean to say that the question whether a man deserves moral praise or blame, or the degree to which he deserves it, depends *entirely* or *always* upon his motive. I think it certainly does not. My point is only that this *question* does *sometimes* depend on the motive, in some degree; whereas the question whether his action was right or wrong *never* depends upon it at all.[18]

In other words, the motive may be important for a decision about moral goodness or badness (sin), but has no part in decisions about the moral rightness or wrongness of acts. In an article published several years after the one we discussed above, Schüller illustrated this point very carefully by taking as an example a physician who develops a new therapeutic device which, he sees, will be beneficial to a very large number of people. The physician, however, is motivated only by selfish ambition. In other words, he does not act out of love for his neighbor, although his achievement, when evaluated by its consequences, is seen to be in accordance with what is required by the commandment of love. Thus his act is morally bad because it is performed from pure selfishness. At the same time, however, it is morally right because of its beneficial consequences.[19]

He clarifies the distinction even further. Suppose, he says, that a certain person feels obliged out of love to help someone. Suppose also that this same person chooses to help, but, by mistake, causes harm. He mistakenly does the opposite of what love demands in deeds. His act is therefore ethically wrong, although it is, at the same time, ethically good "because it springs from the best intentions or inner dispositions."[20]

It will be seen that this terminology has a number of advantages over the scholastic terminology which we discussed above. There is certainly no danger of labelling as a sin an action that is simply not a sin. Indeed, the word "sin" may be used without an adjective and cause no confusion. Moreover, as Schüller points out, the morally right/morally good distinction allows us to formulate in a comprehensible way the teaching that the so-called erroneous conscience obliges morally. The conscience, he says, cannot mislead one about moral goodness and badness. It always and infallibly calls for moral goodness. However, it can mislead one regarding what is morally right. The morality of a person cannot depend upon that person's knowledge, deep or otherwise, of nonmoral elements.[21]

In an article which, up to the time of this writing, has not been published in English translation,[22] Schüller comments upon Knauer's writings, saying that, although the latter speaks of "moral good" and "immoral," he apparently means "morally right" and "morally wrong." Otherwise, says Schüller, he should be reproved.[23]

We have seen, however, that Knauer clearly did not mean morally right and morally wrong. He meant morally good and morally bad (sin). However, in an article published some fifteen years after his original French one[24] (and not yet published in English translation), Knauer does mention the distinction. To say that an action which is not counterproductive is morally right is one thing, but, he asks, is it also for the same reason good, in the proper sense of the word, good before God? He takes the example of someone in a self-service store who does not steal simply because he is afraid of being caught. Obviously, says Knauer, his behavior is morally correct, and he cannot therefore be reproached for committing an evil deed. "But to be good in the strict sense, his action must spring from a good heart."[25]

Knauer has picked an easy example. As he puts it himself, this person's behavior is *obviously* correct. The question remains: can Knauer's brand of proportionalism help a person whose heart is good to work out what is the right thing to do in any set of circumstances? His tendency to concentrate on the *finis operantis* (even though he describes this as, ultimately, a *finis operis*) gives the impression that he is not really interested in working out what is morally right and morally wrong, but only what is morally good and what is morally bad (sin). The problem is highlighted in his reply to another comment of Schüller's. The latter wrote that he saw Knauer's introduction of a distinction between the ethical and the psychological senses of intention as an unnecessary complication. If, for example, we ask under what conditions a nonmoral evil may be caused, the answer is: "when there is a proportionate reason." Thus, in the case of justified punishment (justified by a proportionate reason), the person inflicting the punishment may *intend* the causing of this nonmoral evil because this injury is justified punishment. Any introduction of a distinction between moral and psychological intention is therefore superfluous. Moreover, the concept of moral intention is used in another way, continues Schüller. An executioner, for example, may perform a legitimate execution out of duty, or in order to satisfy his tendency to cruelty. In either case, what he does is morally right, but his morally good intention to do his duty, or his morally bad intention to satisfy his cruel streak is what determines the moral goodness or badness of his behavior.[26]

Knauer's reply is that Schüller's objection is covered by the distinction between *finis operis* and *finis operantis:* if the executioner acts only to satisfy his cruelty (and is not interested in doing his duty), that satisfying of his cruel streak is the *finis operis;* it is, however, the *finis operantis* if he first of all performs the act out of duty but, in addition, wants to satisfy his cruel leanings in this way. Schüller, he says, only confirms the distinction.[27]

However, elsewhere in the same article we find Knauer discussing the concepts of *finis operis* and *finis operantis* with words very similar to those used in his second article. He talks about the *finis operantis* being the *finis operis* of a second act. The act which a person performs has its own *finis operis,* but this act is ordered toward another act, which, in turn, has its own *finis operis.* The *finis operis* of the second act is the *finis operantis* of the first. The judgment of the first act must therefore be modified by taking into account the *finis operantis* (the *finis operis* of the second act).[28] If we apply this reasoning to an example he gives in his second article (that of giving alms in order to gain a tax benefit), we soon see that he is not making clear distinctions. The *finis operantis* is the gaining of a tax benefit. In St. Thomas' example it was the seeking of vainglory. But does the existence of that *finis operantis* mean that giving alms to a person dying of hunger in such a case is morally wrong? Knauer has still not answered that question, and yet it is clear that he sees that proportionalism can be used to work out moral rightness or wrongness, for he actually writes that a person can, after careful examination of the facts, come to the conclusion that a certain action is not counterproductive. However, he points out, it is possible that one day it will be shown to be, "on the whole and in the long run," counterproductive. Only the moral evil of an action can be definitely known, he says, not its moral rightness.[29]

Knauer is correct in asserting that we can be sure we are committing a sin, but are prone to mistakes when working out what is right and what is wrong. Mistakes regarding the moral rightness of actions have, of course, abounded throughout the history of the church—some, like the burning of heretics and the preaching of certain crusades, more glaring than others. It is, therefore, in the area of rightness and wrongness that we need help in order to avoid, or at least reduce, the likelihood of similar disasters in the future. If Knauer restricted proportionalism to that area, the only area in which it is useful, he would have no need to resort to complicated distinctions between psychological and moral intentions, which, probably, very few people outside the ranks of moral theologians and philosophers could understand with any degree of ease.

In an article published in 1977[30] Janssens latched onto the importance of the rightness/goodness distinction. In the end, he wrote, moral goodness and badness are determined by the goodness or badness of a person's disposition or attitude. However, the problem of morality is not limited to the question of moral goodness and badness.

> A good disposition requires us to choose the actions which, in accord with our well considered judgment of conscience, are apt to embody or realise our good attitude. Whether or not our actions are objectively suited to actualise our good disposition is therefore a matter of knowledge and judgment (judgment of conscience) and *ipso facto* of truth or untruth, of rightness or wrongness. That is the reason why we say that an action, which is objectively (in truth) capable of incarnating our good disposition, is morally right, whereas we qualify as morally wrong an action which is inappropriate for that purpose.[31]

However, like Schüller, he goes on to point out that, notwithstanding the essential connection between moral rightness and moral goodness, the distinction between them on the one hand, and between moral wrongness and badness on the other, is extremely important for the simple fact that they do not always coincide.[32]

Fuchs too became convinced of the importance of the distinction, so much so that it has played an important part in several of his most recent works. Just how important a part will become clear as we examine the way (ways) in which the rightness/goodness distinction has been dealt with in the United States.

3. American Proportionalists and the Rightness/Goodness Distinction

In 1973, McCormick produced an interesting paper.[33] It is mainly concerned with the direct/indirect distinction in morals, but, naturally, references to the rightness of acts abound in this work. As it was produced in the early seventies, the lack of a clear distinction between moral rightness and moral goodness throughout its pages should not cause any major surprises. However, the long acceptance of the distinction within certain philosophical circles had not been confined to Great Britain. The American philosopher William Frankena was, therefore, as he put it himself, unhappy with that aspect of McCormick's discussion:

> Like most moral theologians, Catholic and Protestant, he carries his discussion on almost entirely by the use of words like *good, bad, evil in se, value, moral evil, immoral, morally acceptable;* he makes little or no use of *right, wrong, ought, duty, obligation* or *a right.* That is, he mainly uses what I call aretaic terms and only occasionally deontic ones . . . But I must say it seems to me important and even necessary, as V.J. Bourke has recently recognised, 1) to distinguish moral goodness, virtue, and so on as a predicate both of actions and of agents, their motives, character traits and so forth, from moral rightness as a predicate of actions; 2) to take aretaic predicates of actions as dependent on facts and/or aretaic judgments about agents, and so on; and 3) to see deontic predicates of actions as depending, not on the agent's character, intentions, motives and so on, but on an action's nature and/or consequences, that is, on what it consists in, does or sets in train. For actions may be right—do the right thing or what one ought to do—and yet not be morally good.[34]

By the time Frankena wrote this piece, Schüller had already introduced the moral goodness/rightness distinction very clearly into his writing. Not all American proportionalists, however, latched onto it immediately, and, as we shall see, one or two leading proportionalists continued to ignore it even after the publication of Frankena's observations.

In later writings, McCormick himself does seem to display respect for the distinction we are discussing. Here and there, however, his use of the term "moral evil" is rather puzzling. He seems to jump from the level of premoral evil to that of moral evil when he is not discussing sin but wrongful acts. The explanation seems to be given in a comment he makes about an article written by Norbert Rigali. This latter wrote that the term "moral evil" refers to subjective evil, by which he meant "an evil other than that of the moral subject as such."[35] McCormick's reaction is to say that this is not the way the terms "moral evil" and "premoral evil" are used in contemporary writing. They refer instead, he says, to objective rightness and wrongness. Thus moral evil is to be understood in an objective sense as harm which is unjustifiably caused. "Before we know whether it was justifiably caused, it is said to be ontic, premoral, or nonmoral evil."[36] He concludes that in this context the distinction between moral evil and premoral evil has nothing to do with the sinfulness of the person acting.

But is that really how other proportionalists describe the distinction between premoral evil and moral evil? In discussing that very subject,

Fuchs describes moral evils as

> those which, if freely realized, make the human being (as a whole) morally bad. These evils therefore refer to the moral quality of the person, his moral goodness, and are in this sense "intrinsically evil." Examples of such moral evils are . . . the readiness to be unjust, unchaste and unfaithful; also blasphemy, or seducing a person to a sin (that is, to a moral evil). These moral evils which are evils in themselves do not indicate which concrete acts in this world would be a violation of, let us say, justice and chastity; that is, they do not indicate which concrete acts are not morally right and which acts should be realized if a person is to be morally good.[37]

Rudolf Ginters, moreover, whose approach to proportionalism is very similar to Schüller's, describes a moral value as a positive quality of a man (Mensch).[38] Presumably, he would describe a moral disvalue or evil[39] as a negative quality of a person. McCormick's special use of the term "moral evil" is, therefore, somewhat confusing, and would appear to be quite unnecessary. An evil like pain, death or mutilation is, in itself, premoral or nonmoral, and should surely never be described as "moral." It is the act as a whole which is either right or wrong, and it is the person, or the person in his or her acting, who is morally good or morally bad.

In spite of this rather confusing use of the term "moral evil," however, McCormick does, in his most recent writings, display his appreciation of the rightness/goodness distinction. Referring to an article written by Servais Pinckaers on the subject of proportionalism and intrinsically evil acts, he points out that Pinckaers fails to make the distinction. Indeed, says McCormick, he never mentions right and wrong anywhere in the article. He only discusses goodness and badness, involving goodwill, etc. However, continues McCormick, the whole discussion about moral norms is concerned with the rightness and wrongness of concrete human behavior. "To miss this point is to fail to understand the issue."[40]

Another American proportionalist, Philip S. Keane, has also been somewhat confusing in his use of the term "moral evil." He discusses the case in which the agent has a good purpose, but, because of certain circumstances, can achieve that purpose only through the performance of an action "that either contains significant degrees of ontic evil in itself or leads to other results that contain significant degrees of ontic evil." In such cases, he says, "the category of proportionate reason, based on the total concreteness of the action, is the best way to assess whether the ontic evil is also a moral evil."[41] In saying this, Keane seems to be in complete agreement with similar statements made by McCormick. He may also, however, be somewhat influenced by Knauer's writings, as the following piece from a fairly recent article by the same author would seem to indicate:

> When a truly proportionate reason is present in an action so that the action is morally good, the human will is clearly not morally intending the premoral evil in the action, even if the premoral evil must be done as a means to the premoral good. Hence proportionate reason is ultimately a more accurate indicator of what the person is actually doing in a complex human action than is the external structural relationship of the various premoral aspects of the action.[42]

He adds in a footnote:

> Part of the issue here is whether psychological intention is to be distinguished from moral intention. Surely a doctor who amputates a limb to save a person's life has to remove the limb. But does he or she morally intend the evil in the amputation?[43]

For Keane, there is what he calls a "dynamic interrelationship" between proportionate reason and the agent's intending will. An interaction between these two would seem to be a factor, he writes, "in the breakthrough to genuine moral objectivity." He sees as legitimate the traditional concern to distinguish subjective culpability and nonculpability from moral objectivity. However, it may be that sometimes there was "too great a separation between the meaning-giving subject and the realm of moral objectivity." By exploring the relationship between human intending and proportionate reason, we might, he feels, avoid separating them unduly.[44]

The problem in all this, however, would appear to be similar to that which we encountered when we discussed Knauer's writings. Keane seems to be discussing the determination of moral goodness and badness, and simply does not see that proportionalism should be concerned with the determination of the rightness and wrongness of actions.

In an article published in 1981, another leading American proportionalist, Lisa Cahill, confuses what is morally evil with what is morally wrong. She discusses the work of Knauer, Fuchs, Schüller, Janssens and McCormick, and notes that a result of their labors has been the development of a distinction between premoral evil and moral evil or sin. For a good reason, she says, premoral evils may be caused directly, but moral evils may not. The only absolute norms, she goes on to say, regard moral evil, but they are, by necessity, either abstract or stipulate a specific disproportion in the act and circumstances. "Essentially, they affirm that it is always wrong to cause a nonmoral evil for a frivolous or inadequate reason."[45] This last sentence may be considered unobjectionable, but is immediately followed by: "A nonmoral evil (death, pain, error) perpetrated disproportionately is a sin."[46]

Suddenly, we have switched from "wrong" to "sin." Cahill and Keane would have done well to have taken a leaf from a book written by their co-national Timothy O'Connell. He too distinguishes between premoral values or goods and moral values. While, however, he attributes the same meaning to premoral value (good) as they do, his discussion of moral values is quite different from theirs.

> These values differ from those (premoral values) we saw earlier in that they do not so much point "out there" as "in here." They do not name aspects of a particular situation which should be noted and taken into account. Rather they describe qualities of moral persons themselves as they confront and correctly deal with their situations. They describe the kind of persons they should *be*. If we name these values by using adjectives (fair, honest, just, chaste, etc.), then the adjectives are most appropriately modifiers of moral agents themselves. They describe their way of being, they report their success and failure in maximising the premoral good and minimising the premoral evil in a particular area of life. For this reason again, they are called moral values.[47]

O'Connell has latched onto the enormously important truth that lies behind the objection that Fuchs, among others, has to expressions like "material sin."

> This distinction of the past between formal and material sin is not as clear as the distinction we make today between personal evil and material wrongness. For this very reason it is sometimes said that the concept of "only material sin" is an absurdity because sin is precisely a personal evil.[48]

Unfortunately, some of the better known proponents of proportionalism in the United States do not seem to have borne this in mind when producing some of their most influential works. Such being the case, it should not come as a surprise to find that much the same thing is to be found in the opposing camp.

4. The Rightness/Goodness Distinction in the Antiproportionalism Camp in the United States

Apparently preferring what he refers to as the "traditionalist" approach, John Connery compares it to proportionalism. The approach of the traditionalist to the proportionate reason, he says, differs from that of the proportionalist in that the former's main concern is that the evil in the act be *praeter intentionem.* The traditionalist sees the requirement that the good effect be proportionate to the evil one as being meant to guarantee the proper direction of the intention. The morality of the act, says Connery, depends on the intention rather than a weighing of goods and evils.[49]

He illustrates this point with the same clarity, taking as an example the case of someone who uses more violence than is necessary when defending himself against an aggressor. If too much violence is used, he writes, the act is wrong. Now, although St. Thomas does not say so explicitly, he continues, it would seem that the reason for this requirement is related to the intention. The use of more violence than is necessary for the purpose of self-defense implies an intention that goes beyond self-defense (e.g., vengeance or anger). "The injury or killing would hardly remain *praeter intentionem* under these circumstances."[50]

What does Connery mean here when he uses the word "intention"? If the person defending acts out of hatred or revenge, his act is morally bad, but that would be the case even if his defense were *insufficient* to repel the attack of his assailant! Proportionalists are (or, at least in the mind of the present author and in those of a number of the proportionalists so far discussed, should be) concerned with the problem of deciding what is morally right and what is morally wrong. Connery, however, is talking about something else. He is discussing moral goodness and badness. The use of too much violence would be *wrong* regardless of the agent's motivation. It is wrong because it is too much. This is a very important point. What we have concluded is that, in spite of his clarity, Connery has not told us how we are to decide upon the moral rightness or wrongness of an action. He has merely told us that, if our motivation is evil, the act is morally bad. That is true, however, even in the case of morally right acts, as in the case of almsgiving for purposes of vainglory.

William E. May, in an article published as late as 1982, writes that the choice to contracept is "intrinsically disordered, *morally* evil."[51] It may be objected that he probably intended "morally wrong" when he wrote "morally evil." However, some comments in an earlier work written by May and John Harvey would not suggest that such is the case. They discuss the methodology of Fuchs and other authors (apparently including McCormick, Schüller and Janssens among these others).[52] A major problem with such moral methodology, they write, is that, if one adopts it, one can never tell when an act is morally bad. The reason for this lies in the fact that one cannot assume that an act that might be referred to as morally evil is a complete human act, "in the sense in which our authors understand this term," if there is a possibility of the act serving as means to an ulterior good end. What has been judged a morally bad act, they say, might be seen later, after reassessment, to have become part of a larger, morally good act. "According to this theory, even acts that, at some point prior to the moment of choice, are judged to be morally evil, can materially turn into morally good acts by a reassessment of the whole situation."[53] If we were to change those "goods" of May and Harvey into "rights" and their "bads" into "wrongs," we would, I believe, be able to clarify things a little. Everyone agrees that taking food or medicine that belongs to another person is usually wrong. If, however, we add the "ulterior end" of saving somebody's life in an emergency situation, then the act is right. There is, however, never any question of changing personal evil (sin) into moral goodness, or vice versa.[54] May and Harvey appear to be aware of that fact because they write that, according to the moral methodology of Fuchs and others, acts "that, at some point prior to the moment of choice, are judged to be morally evil, can *materially* turn into morally good acts by a reassessment of the whole situation."

However, it would seem that, like so many other people, they have been led, by their own failure to make clear distinctions between rightness and goodness, wrongness and badness, into unnecessary alarm (about sin, one imagines). After all, I am quite sure that they would not be in the least upset by the above example concerning the taking of what belongs to another in order to save a life.

Throughout the debate on proportionalism, a number of scholars in the opposing camp have been influenced by the writings of Germain Grisez.[55] When we come to discuss the direct/indirect distinction, we shall need to make a more detailed examination of his moral theory. For the moment, let it suffice to say that one tenet of that theory is that, in our decision making, we should choose in an "inclusivistic" way. By this he means that where there is a choice between basic goods (life, friendship, aesthetic experience, etc.), we must choose in such a way that the goods not chosen are not positively rejected. Their goodness must be recognized. When we choose in an "exclusivistic" way, that is not the case: before the choice each of the options is recognized as good, but, after the choice, only the chosen option is still seen to be good by the agent, and the others have, in his or her sight, been diminished in their goodness.[56]

As Grisez himself notes, what we are discussing here is an attitude.[57] He would therefore appear to be talking about moral goodness and badness. But, is his analysis correct?

We ought always to choose inclusivistically. For consistent inclusivism in choice is the criterion of moral goodness we have been seeking, whereas moral evil consists in choosing exclusivistically. Indeed, it can be said that no one chooses precisely to *do what is morally wrong;* rather, one *makes choices in a way that is morally wrong*—in an exclusivistic manner."[58]

This is a somewhat surprising statement. Does Grisez *really* mean that nobody chooses to do what is morally wrong? It would appear so. In another, later work, in which he makes it clear that he thinks of Fuchs, McCormick, Janssens, Keane and T.E. O'Connell as consequentialists, he writes:

The condition—that the one about to choose has reached a definite conclusion as to which alternative is preferable in consequentialist terms—requires a knowledge that would preclude a wrong choice.

Why is this so? Because nothing is chosen except insofar as it seems good. If one alternative is seen to promise definitely greater good or lesser evil, the other hardly could be deliberately chosen. What reason or motive could there be to choose the lesser good or the greater evil? In a consequentialist's view of things: None. For in this view, the premoral goodness of the outcome determines the moral rightness of the choice that is a means to it, and the method excludes any other intelligible factor that might tempt a rational agent to choose wrong . . . The point is that if one knew in the way *consequentialism requires* what one ought (on its account of "ought") to choose, one could not choose otherwise.[59]

Grisez's use of terms like "intelligible factor" and "rational agent" are interesting. He seems to be ignoring the fact that morally evil activity (sin) is not reasonable. A sin is a sin not because the agent convinces him- or herself that a certain premoral good is not a premoral good. It is a sin because the agent knows that to reject this good on this occasion is morally wrong. I sin when I freely choose to do what I *know* (or believe) to be morally wrong. The only thing that intelligence can grasp about basic sins, writes Bernard Lonergan, is that there is no intelligibility to be grasped. Basic sin is irrational. If there were a reason for its occurrence, it would not be sin. Although there can be excuses or extenuating circumstances, there cannot be a reason because basic sin consists in failing to yield to reasons. It consists, he continues, "not in inadvertent failure but in advertence and in acknowledgement of obligation that, nonetheless, is not followed by reasonable response."[60]

What Schüller, Fuchs and others are trying to establish is how a reasonable person can work out what is the right (the reasonable) way to act in a given situation. We cannot expect the sinner or the madman to be reasonable.

> The truth is that, if different people are to agree in their ethical judgments, it is not enough for them all to be fully informed. They must all be *reasonable* too. (Even this may not be enough: when it comes to controversial questions, they may reasonably differ.) Unfortunately, people are not always reasonable. And this is a sad fact, which philosophers just have to accept. It is absurd and paradoxical of them to suppose that we need produce a "reasoned argument," for this would be a self-contradiction."[61]

Although Grisez has set himself up as an opponent to proportionalism, he offers no alternative to it, and he most certainly cannot if he continues to hold that one of the problems with proportionalism theory is its claim to enable the moral agent to establish what is right and what is wrong before he makes his choice, thus, according to Grisez, rendering the choice of anything other than the right course of action impossible.

5. What Lies behind the Confusion?

As we have seen, Schüller borrowed the moral rightness/moral goodness distinction from British philosophy. This distinction was also already well known in North American philosophical circles. Why then, were American theologians so slow in picking it up? They could not have been totally ignorant of what was happening among philosophers who spoke and wrote in their language. Why did they have to wait until Schüller, a German theologian, pointed it out to them? The answer to this question could, I think, not only serve to satisfy our curiosity. It could also explain, at least in part, some of the unnecessary anxiety and confusion that we find in the proportionalism debate.

What, then, is the answer? There may indeed be more than one. Many factors may have contributed to the theologians' lack of readiness to accept the philosophers' neat distinction and to the confusion regarding personal goodness and the rightness of an act. One of the major factors, however, would appear to be an inaccurate appreciation of what is contained in the deposit of faith. Theologians and Catholic philosophers who indulge in theology are normally interested in what concerns salvation. We should be more than surprised if they were not. The subject of salvation is, of course, very much bound up with being and becoming morally good. Furthermore, as Fuchs recently pointed out, it is understandable that material moral norms concerning behavior in this world should frequently be understood (mistakenly) to be "truths of salvation" (truths concerning the moral goodness of the person). Why? Because, says Fuchs, in the putting into practice of personal goodness, the personal goodness of the person and the material rightness of the act are found together, or, at least, should be found together. Because personal goodness is a salvific reality, we tend to refer to the whole combination of moral goodness and rightness in an act as a salvific reality, without specifying which element of the whole concrete reality is the truly salvific reality and which is not.[62] This tendency to confuse concrete norms of behavior with truths of salvation has been more than evident in recent times. Ford and Grisez, for example, are of the opinion that there is "an extremely strong case" for saying that what they call "the received Catholic teaching on the immorality of contraception" has been proposed infallibly by the ordinary magisterium. According to them, if we apply what the Second Vatican Council had to say about the infallible exercise of the ordinary magisterium to this case, we see clearly from the history of the way in which the teaching on contraception has been proposed by the church that the criteria for infallibility have been met.[63]

Ford and Grisez say this without in any way arguing against the affirmation that the object of the infallibility of the church has the same extent as the revealed deposit. It extends, they say, to all those things, but *only* to those things "which either directly belong to the revealed deposit itself, or which are required to guard as inviolable and expound with fidelity this same deposit" (*Lumen Gentium,* no. 25).[64] How can the prohibition of a physical act such as artificial contraception, considered in its materiality alone, be described as "belonging to the *depositum fidei* or necessary to guard and expound it?" The infallibility which the church enjoys refers to truths of salvation. Ford and Grisez have failed to make the necessary distinctions. They have apparently assumed that the production of the premoral evil involved in artificial contraception is always morally *wrong.* On that score alone they would run into opposition from the proportionalists. That, however, is not the main point we wish to make here. They then carry their questionable conclusion into the field of what is necessary for salvation.

In this they are far from being unusual. However, let one more example suffice. In an article published in 1981, William B. Smith describes McCormick as the chief American spokesman of the "revision" brought about by Knauer, Fuchs, Schüller et al.[65] Later in the article he quotes no. 62 of *Gaudium et Spes* thus: "For the deposit of faith or revealed truths

are one thing; the manner in which they are formulated without violence
to their meaning and significance is another." Then he adds:

> In my judgment, the "revised" ecclesiology, the "revised" methodology,
> indeed the "revision" of moral theology by Richard A. McCormick honours
> neither the *substance* nor the *formulation* of received Catholic moral teaching
> precisely because his revisionist reformulations do the kind of violence to
> the meaning and significance of Catholic moral teaching that the Second
> Vatican Council enjoined theologians not to do.[66]

Morality in the strict sense, as Fuchs points out, is not directly related
to rightness in our worldly behavior. What it is directly related to is the
person's attitude and, therefore, personal goodness. Moreover, "everything
concerned with this personal attitude concerns salvation."[67] Anything that
concerns salvation is, of course, very much tied up with the deposit of
faith. However, says Fuchs, the admittedly very important question of
right or wrong is not the primary problematic of personal morality, but
the secondary question of what kind of behavior best corresponds to this
innerworldly reality. If we grasp this, we can more easily see that the
solution to problems of right and wrong is neither easy nor uniform.
"Nevertheless, it is not so urgent that it requires the 'absolute,' 'universal,'
'intrinsece malum' character that applies to the realm of good/evil personal
morality."[68] In short, the "revisionist schemes" of McCormick and the
other proportionalists do not in any way alter what is in the deposit of
faith.

Linked to the anxiety resulting from a confusion of truths of salvation
with truths about the rightness and wrongness of actions is a fear of moral
compromise arising from so-called sin-filled situations. Everyone accepts
that we are sometimes forced into the production of premoral evils as a
result of our finitude in time and space. There are, however, other kinds
of situations.

A general enquiry on the state of "popery" (Catholicism) made in Ireland
in 1731 established that in Galway there were nine secular priests, three
friaries, a Jesuit and three nunneries. However, the two city sheriffs later
reported to the mayor that, although they had searched the reputed
Augustinian friary in a certain Back Street, they had not been able to
find any of the friars. Some light is shed on the mystery by an entry in
a surviving account book of the Back Street friary which informs us that,
on November 9, 1731, the "missing" friars spent the sum of one shilling
and one penny on a bottle of wine for the sheriffs. The Dominicans were

apparently more generous. They spent two shillings and two pence "for claret to treat the sheriffs in their search."[69] The bribery or collusion indicated in this story does not shock us at all. Given the anti-Catholic attitude of the government, it seems easy for us to justify the "encouragement" given to the sheriffs to tell untruths and not to do the job they were apparently being paid to do. However, things do not always seem so clear in other "sin-filled situations."[70] Suppose, for example, that a company has to bribe officials in a certain country because everybody else does so, and any company which did not would not get the business it was seeking and would soon find itself in serious financial difficulties. A fear of possible moral compromise in such situations seems to be displayed in an article written by W.B. Smith, who claims that what he calls "revised moral methodology or moral teaching" in practice justifies acts which were never before justified in Catholic moral teaching. Most new discoveries in moral theology, it seems to him, discover only that what was previously called vice in Christian tradition is somehow now justified.[71]

Something similar may lie behind Connery's fear that proportionalism (or, at least, as he put it then, "a morality based solely on consequences"[72]) appears "to call for, or at least allow, exceptions which go against commonly held convictions."[73]

Proportionalists have not always been very effective in alleviating such fears. In a footnote added to the English language edition of his second article, Knauer discusses the case of a woman who could rescue her children from a concentration camp by committing adultery. This difficulty, he says, is by no means limited to the sexual area. The same problem exists in every kind of blackmail or extortion. He gives as an example the case of a man who is threatened with death if he refuses to take part in the falsification of a document. The question, he says, must be seen in relation to the whole context. Then he asks if life or freedom has any value if a person is forced to give up all human rights and be exposed to every kind of extortion. "This would be in contradiction to the very values of life and freedom."[74]

Grisez found this answer evasive "since the question is not regarding extortion in general, but only about a commensurate reason for adultery— not life and freedom, but the recovery of one's children from the clutches of an implacable enemy."[75] It may well be that Knauer himself was moved to this unconvincing reply by his own fear of a moral compromise and the need for a contradiction forced upon him by his own moral theory. Would Knauer really hold that a man capable of forging a passport should not do so for a person who is holding a gun to his head? I think not.

It was to deal with situations of conflict arising from the presence of sin that Charles Curran developed his theology of compromise. In this imperfect world, he says,

> it is never possible to overcome all the effects of sin this side of the eschaton—sometimes one must accept the limitations of the sinful situation. This explains the theological concept of compromise because of which an act which in ordinary circumstances would be wrong for this person in the sinful situation is not wrong.[76]

But is there really any need to speak of compromise? In the correct solution of situations of conflict caused by the presence of sin there is certainly no *moral* compromise. Fuchs notes that limitations on human possibility may sometimes ultimately derive from the sin of the world "on account of the concupiscence of mankind, on account of the objectifications of the 'sin of the world' in society, including situations of injustice, and because of weakness due to the concupiscence of the acting subject."[77] As a result of these limitations, a person may find him- or herself in a situation of conflict the solution of which necessarily involves the sacrifice of a particular value or values in favor of some other value. This sacrifice is forced upon the agent. In individual situations such values do not *absolutely* have to be realized. They are values which are part of the well-being of the human world, but they are not moral values (which must always be implemented). They are instead premoral values "which have to be implemented as far as possible according to the context."[78] In the solution of the conflict, continues Fuchs, we do not have the simultaneous realization of the morally right and the morally wrong. We have only the morally right, "which, however, contains both non-moral right (good/ value) and non-moral wrong (evil/disvalue)."[79]

A hint of discomfort remained in McCormick when he reviewed this article. He noted that, although Fuchs recognized the difference between a compromise occasioned by our sinful situation and one that is rooted in the objective incompatibility of premoral goods, he did not believe that the two can be easily distinguished in practice. In this he thought Fuchs was correct but he also thought that it was important to continue to try to distinguish them because Fuch's use of the terms "premoral" and "nonmoral" to analyze conflicts arising from our sin-conditioned situation was an extension. This extension, he believed, was legitimate, but, in view of the fact that the terms were so badly misunderstood, often distorted and firmly resisted in some quarters, it seemed to him that the analytic gains achieved through them might be threatened unless we continued to try to keep as clear as possible the distinction between what he called "the two types of compromise" and also tried "to tighten our analysis of each."[80]

But is McCormick right in his assertion that Fuchs's use of the term "premoral" in such situations is an extension? Surely, it would be wrong to say that equivalent terminology was not used in such analyses in the past. In the same article in which he comments on Fuchs's paper, McCormick informs us that *malum physicum* was the traditional description of a killing that occurred in a case of legitimate self-defense.[81] But surely, in most cases of legitimate self-defense the violence employed is not necessitated by the finitude of man in space and time. It would be most inconsistent of us to use such terminology in one sin-conditioned situation but not in others.

6. Conclusions to Be Drawn

This chapter has helped to clarify the main issue for us. It has asked the question: what are the proportionalists talking about? It has answered that some of them are talking about how to ascertain the rightness and wrongness of acts, and that it would seem that the others *should* be discussing the same thing, although it is far from clear that they are in fact doing so. Perhaps the factors which impeded American theologians from picking up the rightness/goodness distinction directly from Anglo-Saxon philosophy are still an obstacle for some proportionalists. The absence of this clear distinction in the writings of these last mentioned can have done nothing to convince their opponents about the validity of proportionalism.

A major problem sometimes confronts the good person who is striving to do the right thing, and that problem is: just what *is* the right thing to do in these circumstances? Surely, it is the answer or the way to the answer to this question that proportionalists should be seeking. If what is morally good is what is morally right and what is morally bad is what is morally wrong, we shall have to revise an awful lot of our thinking on moral matters. Some of the people who burned heretics were probably morally good in such actions. Are we to assume, therefore, that the act of burning heretics was morally right? Must rich benefactors seeking admiration stop giving their money to the poor? Surely, they should change their attitude, but continue to give their money.

If a person knows that his or her proposed act is morally wrong, the decision to go ahead and perform that act (that is, the decision not to follow one's conscience) makes that act morally bad (a sin). In the case of a morally right act performed out of hatred, revenge, etc., it is more or less impossible to see the question of proportion coming into the judgment about the moral goodness or badness of the act. In the first case we could say that the act is morally bad because it is performed by a person who knows (or at least believes) that there is no proportionate reason for the premoral evil involved in his or her act. In the second case it is enough to say that the absence of love (agape) makes the act and the person morally bad. In other words, it could be misleading to say that, if we follow Knauer's analysis, proportion (or the lack of it) between the *finis operis* of the first act and the premoral evil involved will tell us whether or not the act is morally right, while proportion (or the lack of it) between the *finis operis* of the more comprehensive act and the premoral evil involved in it will tell us whether or not the act is morally good. What makes an act morally good or bad is the presence or absence of love. This, incidentally, is where proportionalism and situation ethics must part company. Both agree that love (agape), or the lack of it, is the only criterion for moral goodness or badness. Proportionalism, however, if it is to be coherent, cannot accept that love alone makes an action right, although love most certainly demands the pursuit of morally right activity. An action born of love can be wrong, while an action not resulting from love can be right.

Knauer's lack of a clear analysis of the distinction between moral goodness and rightness on the one hand, and moral badness and wrongness on the other, coupled with the absence in the American debate of a proper confrontation between his brand of proportionalism and Schüller's, cannot have helped theologians to see and expound clearly what proportionalism is concerned with. What it must be concerned with is finding out what is right and what is wrong. What really moves a person, his or her real motive, is another matter. Ideally, it is love that moves a person to action. He is a loving person and everything he does is the fruit of love, but love's presence or absence does not tell us whether or not an action is morally right. Love merely encourages, or rather, demands, a sincere search, and surely it is with that search that proportionalism must be concerned.

64 / *Bernard Hoose*

Notes

1. R.H. Dailey, *Introduction to Moral Theology* (New York, 1970), 141.
2. Ibid., 149.
3. Ibid., 150.
4. F.J. O'Connell, *Outlines of Moral Theology* (Milwaukee, 1953), 50.
5. Ibid., 51.
6. P. Knauer, "The Hermeneutic Function. . . ," 14.
7. Ibid., 2.
8. Ibid., 24 (emphasis mine).
9. L. Janssens, "Ontic Evil and Moral Evil," 70.
10. Ibid., 78.
11. Ibid., 57.
12. Ibid., 92, footnote 94.
13. J. Fuchs, "The Absoluteness of Behavioral Moral Norms," 136.
14. Ibid., 137.
15. Ibid., 136.
16. Ibid., 137.
17. B. Schüller, "What Ethical Principles Are Universally Valid?," 24. In the German original Schüller wrote: "Die vorhin formulierte Hypothese bezieht sich nur auf *Handlungsnormen*. Sodann wäre zu fragen, ob und inwieweit wir das Heil und die sittliche Güte eines Mitmenschen unseren Handlungen zum Ziel setzen können. Insofern das der Fall sein sollte, stünden solche Handlungen, da auf den absoluten Wert des Heils und sittlicher Güte bezogen, notwendig unter einer bedingungslosen sittlichen Norm. So könnte eine Handlung, die in der Absicht erfolgte, einen Mitmenschen zu einem Verhalten wider sein Gewissensurteil zu bewegen, schlechterdings durch nichts sittlich gerechtfertigt werden. Kurz, von der Hypothese sind jene Handlungen auszunehmen, die und insoweit sie den sittlichen Wert des Nächsten zum Gegenstand haben" (B. Schüller, "Zur Problematik allgemein verbindlicher ethischer Grundsätze," *Theologie und Philosophie* 45 (1970): 4).
18. G.E. Moore, *Ethics* (London, 1958), 117. (This book was first published in 1912). W.D. Ross also points out that it is not necessary to know the agent's real motive in order to judge on the rightness or wrongness of an act. (See W.D. Ross, *Foundations of Ethics* (Oxford, 1949), 138–39. The first edition of this book appeared in 1939).
19. B. Schüller, "The Double Effect in Catholic Thought: A Reevaluation," in *Doing Evil to Achieve Good,* ed. R.A. McCormick and P. Ramsey (Chicago, 1978), 183.
20. B. Schüller, "Various Types of Grounding for Ethical Norms," in *Readings . . . No. 1,* 191.
21. B. Schüller, *Die Begründung Sittlicher Urteile, Typen Ethischer Argumentation in der Moraltheologie* (Dusseldorf, 1980), 139.
22. B. Schüller, "Neuere Beiträge zum Thema 'Begründung sittlicher Normen'," in *Theologische Berichte IV* (Zurich and Cologne, 1974), 109–81.
23. Ibid., 162.
24. P. Knauer, "Fundamentalethik: Teleologische als deontologische Normenbegründung," *Theologie und Philosophie* 55 (1980): 321–60.
25. Ibid., 358.
26. B. Schüller, "Neuere Beiträge. . . ," 158.
27. P. Knauer, "Fundamentalethik: Teleologische. . . , 347, footnote 28.

28. Ibid., 345.
29. Ibid., 359.
30. L. Janssens, "Norms and Priorities in a Love Ethics," *Louvain Studies* 6 (1977): 207–38.
31. Ibid., 209.
32. Ibid.
33. R.A. McCormick, *Ambiguity in Moral Choice* (Milwaukee, 1973). It was later reproduced in *Doing Evil to Achieve Good*.
34. W.K. Frankena, "McCormick and the Traditional Distinction," in *Doing Evil to Achieve Good*, 146.
35. N.J. Rigali, "Evil and Models of Christian Ethics," *Horizons* 8 (1981): 11.
36. R.A. McCormick, *Notes . . . 1981 through 1984*, 61, footnote 33.
37. J. Fuchs, "An Ongoing Discussion in Christian Ethics: 'Intrinsically Evil Acts'?" in *Christian Ethics in a Secular Arena* (Washington, D.C., and Dublin, 1984), 80.
38. R. Ginters, *Werte und Normen: Einführung in die philosophische und theologische Ethik* (Dusseldorf, 1982), 340.
39. A number of the proportionalists use the word "value" as a synonym for "good," and "disvalue" as a synonym for "evil" in expressions like "premoral good (value)," "moral evil (disvalue)," etc. Paul Quay objected that value and good are not equivalent and that disvalues are not the same as premoral evils. P.M. Quay, "Morality by Calculation of Values," in *Readings . . . No. 1*, 271–75. McCormick, however, replied that, although there may be differences in the dictionary definitions of the words, he, Schüller, Fuchs et al. use the term "value" to mean "an intrinsic good to man, not something that is good simply because it is evaluated as such by human beings" (R.A. McCormick, *Notes . . . 1965 through 1980*, 645). He goes on to say: "If one is going to enter and understand contemporary moral discourse, the terms used must be accepted as the authors use them, not as one thinks they ought to be used" (ibid., 646). See also P.M. Quay, "The Disvalue of Ontic Evil," *Theological Studies* 46 (1985): 262–86, esp. 265, footnote 11 and 281–86.
40. R.A. McCormick, *Notes . . . 1981 through 1984*, 113.
41. P.S. Keane, *Sexual Morality: A Catholic Perspective* (New York, 1977), 49.
42. P.S. Keane, "The Objective Moral Order: Reflections on Recent Research," *Theological Studies* 43 (1982): 275.
43. Ibid., footnote 43.
44. Ibid., 275.
45. L.S. Cahill, "Teleology, Utilitarianism, and Christian Ethics," *Theological Studies* 42 (1981): 611.
46. Ibid.
47. T.E. O'Connell, *Principles for a Catholic Morality* (New York, 1978), 159.
48. J. Fuchs, "An Ongoing Discussion in Christian Ethics: 'Intrinsically Evil Acts'?," 89–90, footnote 5.
49. J.R. Connery, "Catholic Ethics: Has the Norm for Rule-Making Changed?," *Theological Studies* 42 (1981): 249.
50. Ibid., 237–38.
51. W.E. May, "Church Teaching and the Immorality of Contraception," *Homiletic and Pastoral Review* 82 (January, 1982): 17 (emphasis his).
52. Although they specifically refer to Fuch's first contribution, in which Fuchs himself

did not underline the goodness/rightness distinction, it should be pointed out that what we are concerned with here is not what Fuchs said or did not say on that point in that article, but what May and Harvey, writing several years later, had to say about ascertaining moral goodness and badness, rightness and wrongness.

53. W.E. May and J.P. Harvey, *On Understanding Human Sexuality* (Chicago, 1977), 27.

54. Even greater confusion about evil becoming good and good becoming evil is seen in an article from the pen of the Italian theologian, Dario Composta, in which he refers to proportionalists as "consequentialists": "Quando i consequenzialisti si trovano di fronte alle scelte perplesse, dichiarano che l'oggetto preferito rende 'fisico' (detto anche 'premorale,' 'nonmorale') il male che ne deriva; in altre parole, il male che giustificano è 'preferibile' e il bene che non è compiuto (ossia il male che essi approvano) lo chiamano 'fisico,' 'non-morale,' quasicchè si tratasse di un evento estraneo alla volontà. Ma questo ci sembra incredibile: che cioè il male diventi bene (in quanto preferito per 'ragioni proporzionate') e che il bene morale diventi male fisico o 'premorale'! Ciò è contro il buon senso e non è conforme al Vangelo." D. Composta, "Il Consequenzialismo. Una Nuova Corrente della 'Nuova Morale'," *Divinitas* 25 (1981): 152–53.

55. Finnis, Ramsey, and W.E. May all acknowledge a debt to Grisez.

56. G. Grisez and R. Shaw, *Beyond the New Morality* (Notre Dame, Ind., 1974), 93–97. In the introduction the authors state that the ethical theory set forth in the book is, properly speaking, Grisez's.

57. Ibid., 97.

58. Ibid., 96.

59. G. Grisez, "Christian Moral Theology and Consequentialism," in *Principles of Catholic Moral Life* (Washington, D.C., 1981), 298–99.

60. B. Lonergan, *Insight* (London, 1957), 667. A little earlier in the same book he refers to basic sin as a "contradiction of consciousness." The person knows what he ought to do. "If he wills, he does what he ought and diverts his attention from proposals to do what he ought not." But, "if he fails to will, his attention remains on illicit proposals; the incompleteness of their intelligibility and the incoherence of their apparent reasonableness are disregarded" (ibid., 666).

61. S.E. Toulmin, *An Examination of the Place of Reason in Ethics* (Cambridge, 1950), 165. Grisez would appear to be in eminent company in expecting the unreasonable to be reasonable. Toulmin adds the following footnote to the above piece: "I should have thought it unnecessary to formulate such an obvious truth had I not found it overlooked, in practice, by eminent philosophers. For instance, I recall a conversation with Bertrand Russell in which he remarked, as an objection to the present account of ethics, that it would not have convinced Hitler. But whoever supposed that it should? We do not prescribe logic as a treatment for lunacy, or expect philosophers to produce panaceas for psychopaths" (ibid., footnote 2).

62. J. Fuchs, "Moral Truths—Truths of Salvation?," in *Christian Ethics in a Secular Arena* (Washington, D.C., 1984), 52–53.

63. J.C. Ford and G. Grisez, "Contraception and the Infallibility of the Ordinary Magisterium," *Theological Studies* 39 (1978): 312.

64. Ibid., 268.

65. W.B. Smith, "The Revision of Moral Theology in Richard A. McCormick," *Homiletic and Pastoral Review* 81 (March, 1981): 13.

66. Ibid., 2o.

67. J. Fuchs, "Moral Truths—Truths of Salvation?," 63.

68. J. Fuchs, "Teaching Morality: The Tension between Bishops and Theologians within the Church," in *Christian Ethics in a Secular Arena*, 143–44.

69. P.J. Corish, *The Catholic Community in the Seventeenth and Eighteenth Centuries* (Dublin, 1981), 90–91.

70. It is, of course, possible that, although there is certainly moral wrong, there is no sin in the situation. The people in the government agencies may well have thought that their anti-Catholic measures were right. However, we can at least say that certain wrongs pervaded the very atmosphere of Ireland and, of course, Great Britain at that time.

71. W.B. Smith, art. cit., 12–13.

72. We shall discuss this description of proportionalism (made by others as well as Connery) in the next chapter.

73. J.R. Connery, "Morality of Consequences: A Critical Appraisal," 257.

74. P. Knauer, "The Hermeneutic Function. . . ," 39, footnote 24.

75. G. Grisez, *Abortion: The Myths, the Realities and the Arguments* (New York, 1970), 331.

76. C.E. Curran, "Utilitarianism and Contemporary Moral Theology: Situating the Debates," in *Readings . . . No. 1*, 360.

77. J. Fuchs, "The 'Sin of the World' and Normative Morality," *Gregorianum* 61 (1980): 71.

78. Ibid., 73–74.

79. Ibid., 74.

80. R.A. McCormick, *Notes . . . 1981 through 1984*, 10.

81. Ibid., 5.

CHAPTER FOUR

The Teleology/Deontology Distinction

Nowadays proportionalists are often classified as "teleologists," while the majority of their opponents are described as "deontologists," both labels being sometimes modified by the adjective "moderate." Like the rightness/goodness distinction, this terminology had little or no part to play in the early years of the debate. Again, like the rightness/goodness distinction, it seems to have come into the debate as a result of Schüller's excursions into the realm of British philosophy. In order, therefore, to appreciate what is implied in the use of the terms, let us again imitate Schüller and again venture briefly into the world of British ethical philosophy.

1. What Did the Philosophers Say?

Although the fact is seldom mentioned in the debate on proportionalism, the philosophers we are about to discuss belong to a group generally known as the "intuitionists." Among their ranks we find G.E. Moore, whose best claim to fame in the field of ethics is perhaps his coining of the term "naturalistic fallacy." The naturalistic fallacy is often described as the mistake of deriving ought from is, the discovery of which seems to be generally attributed to David Hume. However, as Philippa Foot notes, Hume's name is not to be found in the index of *Principia Ethica,*[1] the book in which Moore launched his attack on the naturalistic fallacy. Julius Kovesi, moreover, objects to the appropriation of *Principia Ethica* "by what we can call the Humean tradition of moral philosophy."[2] Frankena does see a connection between the naturalistic fallacy and the deduction of ought from is. He notes, however, that, although Moore sometimes identifies the one with the other, in the main he holds only that the deduction of ought from is "involves, implies, or rests upon" the naturalistic fallacy.[3]

What exactly, then, did Moore mean by the term "naturalistic fallacy"? And what importance does it have for our discussion? If we were to read only *Principia Ethica,* we should have grounds for thinking that commentators on Moore were right in claiming that, in his opinion, goodness is an indefinable quality which is intuited. We simply know what Good is.[4] Something similar can be said about the color yellow or red, or blue or whatever. Moore, however, does not seem to have been entirely happy with what he wrote about Good and the naturalistic fallacy in *Principia Ethica.* Some years later he wrote:

> In *Principia* I asserted and proposed to prove that "good" (and I think I sometimes, though perhaps not always, was using this word to mean the same as "worth having for its own sake") was indefinable. But all the supposed proofs were certainly fallacious; they entirely failed to prove that "worth having for its own sake" is indefinable: And I think perhaps it is definable: I do not know. But I also still think that very likely it is indefinable.[5]

Moore had given expression to his uncertainty on this point some years earlier in an unpublished and unfinished preface to a proposed second edition of *Principia Ethica,* which did not materialize. C. Lewy recounts some of the contents of that preface in an article published in 1970.[6] There Moore says that he still thinks that it is probably true that Good is simple in the sense of being indefinable or unanalyzable, but he is not certain, "for it seems to him that possibly 'right' is unanalyzable, and Good is to be analyzed partly in terms of 'right'."[7] However, the fact that it is or is not analyzable no longer seems so important to him. It would be a mistake to suppose, as he had done in *Principia Ethica,* that the fact that Good is not identical with any such property as "is desired" or "is a state of pleasure" rests on the contention that Good is unanalyzable. What he had really wanted to say was that "Good was not identical with any natural or metaphysical property."[8] To explain better what he meant by that, he proposed the following definitions:

> A natural property is a property with which it is the business of the natural sciences or psychology to deal, or which can be completely defined in terms of such. A "metaphysical" property is a property which stands to some super-sensible object in the same relation in which natural properties stand to natural objects.[9]

He found a certain amount of confusion in his discussion of the naturalistic fallacy in *Principia Ethica*. He therefore states in the preface that, if he still wished to use the term, he would define it as follows:

> "So-and-so is committing the naturalistic fallacy" means "He is *either* confusing Good with a natural or metaphysical[10] property *or* holding it to be identical with such a property *or* making an inference *based* upon such a confusion."[11]

And Moore would also expressly point out that, in so using the term "fallacy" he was using it in an extended, and perhaps improper, sense.[12]

Philippa Foot writes that Moore's central thesis "was that goodness is a simple non-natural property discovered by intuition."[13] From what we have just seen, it would appear that Moore himself was not convinced about goodness being simple. However, if we attach no importance to that adjective and stretch "natural" to include "metaphysical," it would seem that we have here a fair statement of the basis of Moore's ethical theory. The word "basis" is carefully chosen, for, as Foot again points out, the rest of Moore's ethics is built upon that foundation.[14] Right action, in his scheme of things, is that which produces the greatest amount of good on the whole. It seems self-evident to him, he says, that our duty is "to do what will produce the best effects *upon the whole,* no matter how bad the effects upon ourselves may be and no matter how much good we ourselves may lose by it."[15]

John Hill describes Moore's ethics thus: "right actions were explained in terms of good things, and good things were explained in terms of Good."[16] That brings us very naturally (if I may be permitted to use such a dangerous word) to the subject of teleological theories and how they differ from deontological ones. We shall begin with the latter. Deontological theories, says C.D. Broad,

> hold that there are ethical propositions of the form: "Such and such a kind of action would always be right (or wrong) in such and such circumstances, no matter what its consequences might be". . . . Teleological theories hold that the rightness or wrongness of an action is always determined by its tendency to produce certain consequences which are intrinsically good or bad.[17]

Now, Moore claims that one cannot find a conclusive reason against the view that his theory is correct insofar as it holds that the rightness or wrongness of an action always depends on its *actual* consequences. He sees no sufficient reason for holding that it depends on the intrinsic nature of the action or on the motive or even on the *probable* consequences.[18] Moore's ethical theory would therefore certainly seem to have something of a teleological character about it. Not all intuitionists, however, agree with his basic approach. Probably the most famous and the most influential of those who disagreed with him during his own lifetime was W.D. Ross, who is generally described as a "deontologist." Moral theories based on consequences, writes Ross, can be either naturalistic or nonnaturalistic. Anyone, for example, who defines "right" as "productive of the greatest pleasure" is advocating a naturalistic definition, while anyone who defines "right" as "productive of the greatest amount of good" is advocating a nonnaturalistic definition.[19] Moore's attempt to define "right" in a nonnaturalistic way (as "productive of the greatest possible amount of good") was the only one known to Ross. He was most decidedly opposed to it.[20] He saw "morally right" as an indefinable characteristic. It could be held to be a wider relation, such as suitability, he wrote, but its differentia can be stated only by the phrase "morally right" or by a synonym of "morally right." Something similar applies to the color red. One can only indicate what distinguishes it from other colors by describing it as the color that is red.[21]

We grasp the general truths, he says, by intuitive induction, as we do in mathematics. We see, for example, that a particular imagined act would produce pleasure for another person, and that, as such, it has a claim on us. From this it is a short step, and an inevitable one, to seeing that any act which has the same constitutive character would possess the characteristic of *prima facie* rightness. We cannot, however, claim intuitive certainty, or indeed any other kind of certainty, regarding the actual or resultant rightness of a particular act.[22] With regard to the problem of working out which of the *prima facie* duties which present themselves in a case of conflict is our actual duty, Ross says that "when we are dealing with obligations of the same kind we have certain criteria for measuring their obligatoriness." In such cases we see that, all things being equal, we have a greater *prima facie* obligation to produce a great good than to produce a small one. We also see that we have a greater *prima facie* obligation "to fulfill a very explicit and deliberate promise, than to fulfill one which is casually made and not taken very seriously by the promisee." However, a problem arises when we try to balance a *prima facie* obligation to produce a certain good against a *prima facie* duty to fulfill a certain promise. Here, says Ross, "we move in a region of uncertainty." In some cases, most men agree, but in others they are more or less evenly divided, and each one can say only: "this *seems* to me to be the right course."[23]

On comparing this with Broad's definition of deontological theories, one might feel that there is little here to justify Ross's being described as a deontologist, for, in Ross's scheme of things, norms like "do not break promises" and "do not take what belongs to another without his or her permission" are merely *prima facie* duties. In cases of conflict, one's actual duty may involve breaking a promise or taking what belongs to another without permission, or both. One might also feel that, regardless of how the two scholars themselves saw things, in any particular case, the results would be the same whether one applied Moore's theory or Ross's, and that the process involved in choosing the right action would be more or less the same in both systems. Let us take a concrete example from the history books. An Act of Parliament passed in England in 1585 ordered all Catholic priests ordained after June 1559 to leave the country. Those who remained in England after a certain date were to be put to death as traitors, and laypeople who harbored or assisted them were to be hanged as felons.[24]

Let us suppose that a priest is hiding in Mr. Castle's house. A government agent calls at his house and asks: "Are you hiding a Catholic priest here?" If we were to apply Moore's reasoning in such a case, we would have no difficulty in deciding that the most good, or perhaps we should say, the least harm, would be produced by telling an untruth. Even if we wish to quibble over the difference between probable and actual consequences, we are quite sure what the actual consequences of telling the truth would be. So we conclude that the right action for Mr. Castle in this case is for him to deny that he is hiding a priest. If, on the other hand, we were to apply Ross's reasoning, we would see that, although there is a *prima facie* duty to tell the truth, Mr. Castle's actual duty is to protect the priest and himself by telling an untruth. The lack of a neat distinction between Ross's so-called deontology and Moore's teleology seems even more evident when we examine what really happened in sixteenth century England. In practice, the English Catholics came up against a real deontological norm. Up to that time most of the great theologians in the church had followed St. Augustine in teaching that a man should not tell an untruth even to save his neighbor's life.[25]

The complete lack of regard for consequences involved in the acceptance of such a norm could lead to truly amazing situations.[26] Suppose, for example, that an enemy soldier who is out to kill your friend asks you if he is hiding in your house. You do not say "no" because you accept that telling an untruth with the intention of deceiving your neighbor can never be justified, so you say "yes." The man then goes into your house and attacks your friend (an unarmed, badly wounded soldier). You are, of course, entitled to go into the house and protect your friend, using against his aggressor whatever force is appropriate, even going so far as to blow his brains out, if that is absolutely necessary. And if the enquiring soldier is accompanied and assisted by others in attacking your friend, you may blow all of their brains out, always provided, of course, that such violence is necessary. Such an act would be legitimate defense of a third party, and the tradition of Catholic moral theology down through the centuries would uphold the legitimacy of your act. But, of course, you might have been able to avoid all that bloodshed by telling a little untruth.

It is hard to imagine Ross condoning such an appalling state of affairs. The duty to tell the truth without any reference to a specific context could never be more than a *prima facie* duty in Ross's scheme of things. Ross, then, does not seem to have been a deontologist in anything like the sense in which some Catholic theologians have been and are deontologists (although only in very limited areas). Ross, however, did have what he saw to be good reasons for objecting to Moore's theory. There are, he said, several branches of duty which it seemed to him could not be grounded on productivity of the greatest good. Examples are the fulfilling of promises, the duty of making compensation for our wrongdoings, the duty of rendering a return for services received. We are aware of the fact that we have duties to behave in these ways even when we are not convinced that the greatest amount of good will be produced by behaving thus. This is so even if we take more distant consequences into account. In the case of promise keeping, for example, we are aware of our duty even when the secrecy of the promise prevents an increase in general mutual confidence resulting from its being kept. We are, moreover, aware of our duty to do what is just, and justice, he notes, does not refer to the production of the greatest sum of good but to the right distribution of good.[27]

Given his opinion about *prima facie* duties, we may safely assume, it would seem, that Ross would not say that promises must always be kept, regardless of consequences. For example, suppose that I have promised John that I will not tell Tom that he is going to visit him. I later discover that John intends to kill Tom. In such a case the *prima facie* duty of keeping the promise will surely give way to the duty to warn Tom of John's intentions. However, the substance of Ross's argument is not so easily dismissed. Perhaps a little explanation from his own writings would be useful.

In certain circumstances we do not in fact think our duty is to do that act which seems likely to produce most good. When we have promised to confer a certain benefit on another person, we do not think it self-evident that we ought rather to confer a greater benefit, if we can, on someone else; we think that the person to whom we have made a promise has a claim on us, just because we have given our promise, which makes it right to confer the promised benefit on him rather than an equal or slightly greater unpromised benefit on someone else.[28]

Some years ago O.A. Johnson wrote regarding deontological theories that, if rightness and goodness are really so independent of each other that one may have fulfilled his duty even though what he has done leaves the world a worse place than it would have been if he had not performed the act, then it seems that moral action becomes irrational and that ethics becomes impossible.[29]

These comments seem to be valid enough when applied to such deontological norms as the above-mentioned ban on the telling of untruths. They would not seem to be applicable, however, in the case of W.D. Ross. After all, if consistency is to be preserved in his scheme of things, even promise keeping and justice must be placed in the category of *prima facie* duties which may or may not be actual duties in particular cases.

2. Where Does Proportionalism Fit in?

It is easy to see that there are similarities between the debate in Anglo-Saxon philosophical circles which we have just discussed very briefly and the debate on proportionalism. The proportionalists are, in fact, called teleologists by themselves and by their opponents. Some of their opponents, inasmuch as they uphold the validity of absolute norms similar to the aforementioned ban on the telling of untruths, could well be (and are) described as deontologists, in some areas at least. These Catholic deontologists, however, bear hardly any resemblance to most of the so-called deontologists found in the philosophy debate.[30] Indeed, it would seem that the latter, if they followed the reasoning of Ross, would have to conclude that the deontological norms found in Catholic moral theology are based on the naturalistic fallacy. If, then, it is misleading to put the Catholic deontologists into the same category as W.D. Ross, is it or is it not misleading to put the proportionalists into the same category as G.E. Moore and call both him and them consequentialists?

(a) *Consequentialism or Proportionalism?*   It is hardly surprising that scholars in the opposing camp should have labelled proportionalism as "consequentialism." The name of Milhaven is often associated with the proportionalists, and Milhaven unashamedly entitled his 1971 article "Objective Moral Evaluation of Consequences." In the early days of the debate, moreover, the proportionalists apparently saw no danger in describing themselves and their colleagues as consequentialists. Hence, in 1972, we find McCormick introducing his review of Fuchs's article on the absoluteness of moral norms with the words: "Josef Fuchs, S.J., has written a lengthy study which appears to contain a significant shift in his methodology toward a morality of consequences."[31] When, however, John Connery reviewed the work of the same Fuchs along with that of Schüller, Knauer and others, and concluded that they were "tending toward consequentialism,"[32] McCormick was not happy. Later, he was not at all unhappy when Franz Böckle declared that a large group of moral theologians was convinced that moral norms concerned with the interhuman area can only be grounded teleologically, "that is, exclusively through a consideration of the foreseen consequences of the action."[33] McCormick himself throws light on the apparent contradictions found here. In recent writing, he says, the term "consequences" means that all things must be considered before a judgment of rightness or wrongness can be made. When authors say that all things must be considered, they are not referring to total net good in the sense of mere welfare values. "The usage 'total net good' (or evil) too easily excludes from consideration factors that go into determining proportion (expressive actions—dignity values—institutional obligations, etc.)."[34] Elsewhere he says that recent Catholic revisionists, including himself, "insist that elements other than consequences function in moral rightness and wrongness."[35] It is clear from a footnote on the same page, however, that the other elements include "the distinction between instrumental acts, actions having a meaning in themselves, and expressive action; the institutional character of some actions; the *ordo bonorum* and *ordo caritatis.*"[36] In short, it all depends on what you mean by "consequences."

With this in mind, we can now return to McCormick's objection to Connery's statement that the approach of Schüller, Fuchs, Knauer et al. is based *solely* on consequences. McCormick indicates that his objection arises from Connery's apparent understanding of consequences as "intended consequences," as though the rightness or wrongness of the action were determined by the intention alone.[37] That, he points out, is not what the authors under discussion are saying. They would all admit, for example, that there is an inherent value in keeping secrets and an inherent disvalue in revealing them. The question is not that the revealing of secrets is wrong because of bad consequences. Breaking secrecy is recognized as a disvalue. The question, therefore, is: when is it legitimate to bring about that disvalue and why? The authors under discussion insist that the revelation of secrets is a premoral evil. They are not, therefore, talking about consequences alone. What they are discussing is the proportion between the evil involved and the good that is being sought. If, however, they saw the rightness or wrongness of the action as based on consequences alone, they would see the revelation of secrets as neutral, not as a premoral evil.[38]

I am not at all sure that McCormick dealt very fully with the problem of consequences meaning only "intended consequences" when he wrote the above piece. Thereafter, Connery refrained from accusations of consequentialism when referring to Knauer, Fuchs and the others, and adopted the term "proportionalism." In explaining his reasons for doing so, however, he does not show signs of having been totally satisfied on the issue of intended consequences being those which count. He writes in a footnote that he had in a previous article identified proportionalism with consequentialism. Here he says that he still sees proportionalism and consequentialism as presenting the same problem, i.e., they both deny the possibility of "an independent morality deriving from the object of the act." However, he admits that it is more accurate to say that proportionalism involves an assessment of all the good and evil in an act and not just the consequences. "Even when proportionalists speak of an act getting its morality from the *finis* or end (the intended consequence), they still call for a proportion between the means and end, and, presumably, other unintended consequences."[39]

All might appear to be well, but Connery adds in a second footnote that he gets the impression that some proportionalists often take a shortcut in the process of making a moral judgment of an act, the criterion of proportionate reason being applied only to the intended effect. Thus the act is judged to be morally good (does he mean "right"?) if the intended good outweighs the evil means, little or no attention being given to the other effects of the act. Unintended effects, he concludes, play a less important role in a system in which moral judgment is closely linked to intention.[40]

Not surprisingly, perhaps, he adds further on in the same article that many proportionalists seem willing to say simply "that it is permissible to do evil to achieve a good purpose." However, says Connery, "some means have a morality of their own and a good end will not justify them."[41]

Referring to this article, McCormick wrote that Connery sees proportionate reason as synonymous with end or motive, and thus interprets proportionalists as holding that "proportionate reason is something *in addition* to a clearly definable action."[42] In his reply Connery said that he did *not* assume that proportionate reason was synonymous with intention. In his article he had merely been critical of proportionalists who used a teleological shortcut, since, according to their own methodology, they should have taken into account all the good and evil contained in the act. However, continues Connery, McCormick's real cause for complaint arises from the fact that he considers proportionate reason to be part of the object of the act. He (Connery) had therefore been wrong in claiming that proportionalists deny that an act can be morally wrong *ex objecto.* The key to the solution to this problem, he says, seems to lie in the meaning of the word "object." It is possible for that word to include object, end and circumstances.[43] If the proportionate reason extends to all the good in the act, and not just the end or motivation, it should apparently include all the other circumstances of the act, but if we thus include the proportionate reason in the object, the whole act is reduced to object. This has been done, says Connery, but when it is done the claim that an act can be right or wrong *ex objecto* does not mean a great deal. "To say that an act is morally definable *ex objecto* is not saying much if it simply means that the whole act is morally definable."[44]

Much of the rest of their discussion was devoted to the possibility of using the term *materia circa quam* to mean "object" in the narrow, restricted sense, and there is even a mention of the possibility that traditional terminology might not be adaptable to proportionalism. That, however, does not seem to get to the bottom of all the issues. One of the issues, of course, is the possibility that an action may be described as intrinsically evil in its materiality alone, regardless of ends and circumstances. We shall deal with that in the next chapter. However, another problem arises from the discussion between McCormick and Connery, and that cannot wait. If the object of an act includes motivation, we are back to the problem we discussed in the third chapter. Can a sin be defined from the object of an act? When we refer to the rightness or wrongness of an act, we refer to the right or wrong solution to a particular problem or the suitability of an act in a particular case. In short, is it or is it not what is required in this situation? If a strong man, well trained in the martial arts, sees a much weaker man strangling a child, the situation demands the nonmoral evil of violent intervention (appeals like "please don't do that" being worse than useless). The nonmoral good of saving the child's life is a proportionate reason. The act, therefore, is right (provided, of course, that the strong man uses no more violence than is necessary). It is, however, possible that the strong man's motive for acting is his desire to be admired by the child's older sister. That motive is important when it comes to a judgment on the level of moral goodness or badness, but has nothing to do with the rightness of the act. The strong man's violent intervention is just what is required. We can certainly, therefore, include saving the child in the object of the act, along with the circumstances and the object in the narrow sense (disabling the child's assailant), and thus say that the rightness of the act is determined by its object (in the fuller sense), if we wish to continue using that terminology. Goodness or badness, however, cannot be determined in the same way. That is why we should not include in the object the motive (in the sense of what really moves the agent: is there only a desire to impress and no love?).

Having said all that, we have not yet dealt with Connery's concern about proportionalists' using the end or intention as a short cut in moral judgments. Does he have any grounds for such fears? Cahill, who describes proportionalism as a teleological theory, says that the term "teleological" is derived from the Greek word τελοζ meaning "goal."[45] She then describes teleology as a "view which models human agency on the pursuit of an appropriate ultimate goal—whether it be happiness or union with all persons in God—and of intermediate goals subsidiary to it."[46] Now, it would be foolish to disagree with Cahill's translation of the word τελοζ as "goal." Aristotle clearly uses it in that sense in his *Nichomachean Ethics,* and, for that reason, is well described by his various commentators as a teleologist. The problem with the word τελοζ, however, lies in the fact that, like the English noun "end," it is ambiguous (even "polyguous"). It can also mean "end achieved," "completion," "result," "consequence" (and various other things which do not concern us here). Goals, of course, often become results or consequences of one's actions. The problem, however, is that they are not always the only consequences. Cahill and other proportionalists who would agree with her definition of teleology are, in practice, interested in consequences other than goals achieved, and would therefore have some sympathy with Broad's description of teleological theories as those that "hold that the rightness or wrongness of an action is always determined by its tendency to produce certain consequences which are intrinsically good or bad."[47] Not all the consequences (even the foreseeable ones) will coincide necessarily, or even probably, with the aims of the agent.

While, therefore, Cahill is certainly not wrong in her definition of teleology (in one of its meanings), some confusion over the ambiguity contained in the words "teleology" and "teleological" could lead some people to think that proportionalists attribute too much importance to the end or intention (or even the motive) when making judgments about the rightness or wrongness of an act. In other words, if we are to go on calling proportionalism a teleological theory, we must state clearly that in the proportionalist "calculation" not only the end or intention, but also all foreseeable consequences are taken into consideration. As for Cahill, we shall see a little later that her own teleology does in fact seem to involve a combination of both meanings of the word τελοζ (goal and consequence).

It should also be made clear that the word "consequences" can be misleading. McCormick, we have seen, gives it a much broader meaning than "total net good" (or evil) in the sense of the total of welfare values (or disvalues), and, clearly, it should have this meaning if it is to be applied to proportionalism. However, it may seem to some that "consequence" is not a fitting label for everything that is contained in the proportionalist "calculation." And indeed, precisely because it is sometimes used as a label for everything contained in the "calculation," some observers may be led to believe that the very meaning itself of an action is not taken into account, since the consequences of an act are usually understood to be other than the act of which they are consequences. It should therefore be stated quite clearly that the meaning of the action is most certainly taken into account.

Some of the dangers inherent in the use of the term "consequences" are made more evident in a recently published article by Joseph Seifert. If, he asks, only consequences are decisive for the moral value of an act, why are animal or natural causes not morally good when they produce life or the happiness of persons?[48] The question, however, is surprising. Moral theology and philosophical ethics are concerned with persons. We judge as morally right or wrong the action that a reasoning *person* intends. That person and the action are morally good if the action is performed out of love. Now, whatever the merits or demerits of talking about the intentions and the love of volcanoes and hamsters, the "duties" of such beings are simply not the subject matter of moral theology. Seifert, of course, knows this. He seems to be led to raise the question only because he thinks that, in proportionalism (although he does not use that word), the agent is not really important "because all that counts are the *effects* of his actions, not the actions themselves qua personal acts and the conscious intentions."[49] He obviously has not noticed that what is important in proportionalism is the proportionate *reason* that a person (the agent) has or does not have. The proportion, moreover, is not merely proportion between the good reason and the bad effects. Other things, as we have seen, must be taken into account. One of those things is the very meaning of the act.

(b) *Calculating Proportion*   One of the most important elements in the proportionalist calculus, and one which we have not yet discussed in any depth, is that all-important proportion between the various premoral goods and evils involved in the action. Just how is that proportion calculated? There has been more than one reply from the proportionalists. That fact alone might be enough to indicate that some difficulty lies ahead. Our main problem, however, is not that there is a mere difficulty involved in the calculation of proportion. Right at the beginning of the debate an *impossibility* was introduced. It will be recalled that, although he retained the direct/indirect terminology, Knauer effectively reduced the number of conditions in the principle of double effect from four to one: the need for a proportionate or commensurate reason. He was well aware of the fact that, having done so, he could be accused of leaving the moral agent with an impossible calculation to work out. How is it possible to compare things which have little or nothing in common? Is Beethoven's Fifth Symphony better than the Mona Lisa? Is the Pietà better than both of them? Which, if any, of them is preferable to a hamburger with tomato ketchup?

To make matters worse, the terms "proportion" and "commensurate" have a ring of mathematics about them. Yet we do in fact often use language which implies calculations in contexts that have little to do with mathematics, and I am not referring exclusively to the field of ethics. Let us, for example, suppose that Mary is afraid of the dark. An unfeeling psychologist who is researching such phenomena places her in a small, well-lit room in an old castle. There is no food in the room. In order to eat she must leave the castle, but the only way out is through a large hall in which there is no lighting of any kind. To cross it she must carry a lighted candle. After two days Mary leaves the well-lit room, crosses the dark hall and comes out into the sunlight. The psychologist asks her: "Why did you go into the dark hall? Weren't you afraid?" "Yes," she replies, "but I was more hungry than afraid." We understand what Mary says, but what kind of calculation has she made? Just how much more hungry? Was the strength of her hunger three times greater than the strength of her fear or just 1.2 times greater? These questions make no more sense than those we asked about Beethoven's Fifth Symphony, the Mona Lisa, the Pietà and hamburgers, and yet, what Mary says does contain some sense. There is a "more" involved, but how do we calculate it? The same kind of problem occurs in ethics when we come to talk about proportion. If we simply say that the premoral good achieved must outweigh the premoral evil that is produced along with it, we give ourselves a problem which looks very similar to problems about hunger outweighing fear. That is why Knauer began talking about an impossibility so early in the debate about proportionalism: "Such a *quantitative* comparison is not possible, as it is a matter of *qualitatively* different values which cannot be compared with one another."[50]

In an attempt to overcome the problem, Knauer turns to Aquinas. Thomas, he points out, said that the whole act must correspond to its end. "End" here means "the reason for the act." The act must therefore correspond to the reason for the act. Now, to say that the reason for an act must be commensurate to the act itself, continues Knauer, is the same as saying that the act must correspond to its reason. When an act is contradictory to the fullest achievement of its end "in relation to the whole of reality," it is immoral. "A short run 'more' of the value is paid by a 'lesser' achievement of the same value in the long run."[51]

Obviously, another way of saying that an act is contradictory to the fullest achievement of its own end is to say that the act lacks coherence. At first glance, therefore, it might appear that Knauer has overcome the problem of reducing proportionalism to impossible mathematical calculations. His thesis, however, is not without its own problems. In commenting upon it, Schüller notes that there are two kinds of contradiction: 1) when too high a price is set on a certain value; 2) when the price set on a value is so high that it is impossible to attain that value. In the second case we have a serious error of logic concerning intention. This is what Knauer is talking about when he refers to a contradiction between means and end. In the first case, however, we have an erroneous assessment of one value when compared to another. If someone says, for example, that the value of a work of art such as a statue of Phidias outweighs the misery of all the millions of slaves in ancient times, as H. von Treitschke apparently once did, the error does not lie in the fact that, in the long run, slavery would hinder rather than promote the production of masterpieces. The error lies rather in the fact that somebody is prepared to pay such a monstrous price for a statue of Phidias. Knauer, it seems, says Schüller, wants to take one very important way of determining moral rightness and make it the universal way. It is probably possible, he continues, to define freedom from contradiction in intending in such a way that it does, in fact, determine well enough the moral rightness of any way of acting. However, we should not expect freedom from contradiction defined in such a way to be any more helpful than a principle such as the one that states that the lesser of two evils should be chosen.[52]

In his reply to these observations, Knauer maintains that both situations boil down to the same thing. In one, he says, we have the lack of a proportionate reason making the omission of the promotion of another value illicit, while, in the other situation, the action is in the same way illicit because the reason for it is not proportionate. If, in the pursuit of one value, we sacrifice another value, and such a sacrifice is not necessary, then the loss of that value is directly intended and establishes the action as counterproductive. Taking the loss into the bargain "is, as it were, a diminution of the value itself."[53]

But is Knauer really convincing here? Just how do we establish that the loss of a value is necessary or not? If counterproductivity is so hard to pin down, are there really any advantages in accepting it as the universal measure of proportionality? Perhaps one or two examples will help to illustrate the problems in Knauer's scheme of things. Suppose that John's young son does something naughty and has done the same naughty deed many times. John judges that, for his own good, his son must be punished. In normal circumstances he would have no difficulty in justifying the premoral evil involved in the act of punishment. The means would be proportionate to the end, and no other premorally evil elements in the action itself or in the foreseeable consequences would be sufficient to render the punishment unjustifiable. However, John's aunt is staying in his house for a week, and today is Friday the thirteenth day of the month. She is very superstitious and a little unbalanced. She is convinced that punishment inflicted on a child on Friday the thirteenth brings disaster on the household in which it occurs. If John punishes his son she will most certainly get to know about it. Rather than cause his aunt sleepless nights and panic-filled days, John decides not to punish his son on this occasion. He has weighed the premoral evils involved against each other. If he does not punish his son, the boy will most certainly perform that naughty deed again. He judges, however, that, in comparison to the disastrous effect that the punishment would have upon his aunt, the certain repetition of the naughty deed is the lesser of the premoral evils. Now, in this case, can we really claim that the means (punishment) was in contradiction to the end (education of the child)? John may even be sure that his son would not get to hear about the effect that this punishment would have upon his great aunt.

Some people might feel inclined to object at this point that this story, far from illustrating the strength of Schüller's objection to Knauer's thesis, merely illustrates the fact that the present author has a lively imagination. They might feel that it is unfair to discuss cases in which the production of the relevant premoral evils is dependent upon the probable reaction of a person other than the moral agent. However, a large amount of our decision making is done under such conditions. For the sake of variety, let us take a rather unusual example from real life. The example chosen concerns the founder of psychoanalysis, Sigmund Freud.

> Freud was a member of both the British and American S.P.R. (Societies for Psychical Research), and in 1924 wrote to Ernest Jones that he was prepared "to lend the support of psychoanalysis to the matter of telepathy." But Jones feared that this would discredit psychoanalysis and dissuaded Freud from any public gesture. He also prevented Freud from reading at the International Psychoanalytic Congress in 1922, an essay he had prepared on "Psychoanalysis and Telepathy." It was only published after Freud's death.[54]

In this case Freud and Jones were both apparently convinced that psychoanalysis had a great deal to give to mankind, and both were apparently equally convinced of the need for a serious attitude toward research regarding telepathy. I suppose we may assume that at that time (and perhaps even today) many people were of the opinion that telepathy was to be classified along with beliefs that vampires and werewolves abound when the moon is full. Obviously, a certain amount of caution was called for. If Freud had declared openly that he took telepathy seriously, he would probably have caused a number of people to sit up and take notice, but he would also very likely have caused a very large number of people to dismiss his not very easy to accept ideas on psychoanalysis as the mumblings of an idiot, or, at best, the expression of one man's eccentricities.

Freud and Jones, then, were not concerned, it would seem, that the promotion of research into telepathy in this way might hinder such research in the long run. On the contrary, telepathic research stood only to gain. It was the likely damage to the progress of psychoanalysis which dissuaded them from such promotion. We could perhaps force Knauer's ideas on counterproductivity into the picture by saying that, in the long run, scholarly research would have been hindered by such promotion of scholarly research. But what help would that be? At some stage Freud and Jones had to decide which was more important, the promotion of the cause of telepathy or the damage likely to be done to the cause of psychoanalysis. In other words, the various premoral goods and premoral evils had to be weighed against each other.

Bearing all of this in mind, let us now return to the debate in America. McCormick has certainly been influenced considerably by Schüller's writings in recent years. In spite of that fact, however, we find in some of his own writings a heavy accent on the importance of counterproductivity. In 1973 he wrote that an action is disproportionate "if a lesser value is preferred to a more important one; if evil is unnecessarily caused in the protection of a greater good; if in the circumstances, the manner of protecting the good will undermine it in the long run."[55] Later he revised his ideas regarding the importance of "the long run." In *Ambiguity in Moral Choice* he had taken the example of the direct killing of noncombatants in a war and had said that it was the long-term effects that constituted its decisive immorality, adding that those effects were traceable to directness itself.[56] Although he still felt that disproportionate actions, like unnecessary harm, could be expected to have "deleterious long-term effects," he no longer saw those effects as the determinants of wrongfulness in such cases. Wrongfulness, he continued, has to be attributed to a lack of proportion, by which he meant that the value being sought "is being pursued in a way calculated in human judgment (not without prediscursive elements) to undermine it." He also tentatively sought to explain the disproportion in terms of an association of basic goods, suggesting that the way in which a good is protected or sought can bring other goods into play and be responsible for disproportion as a result.

In a recently published article, Brian V. Johnstone examines McCormick's idea of an association of basic goods, but finds it unsatisfactory. He takes up the example of protecting human life by causing serious injury to liberty. In McCormick's scheme of things, the undermining of liberty would amount to the undermining of life itself because liberty is an associated good upon which the good of life itself depends. There is, notes Johnstone, no attempt at establishing an abstract hierarchy of values in all this. Instead, a value is ordered to another one as a necessary condition for its realization, and this, he says, provides a basis for a meaningful comparison. However, to find out whether or not an act has such an undermining effect on the value of life, we should need some kind of long-term calculation of effects which "would call for such a complex and hypothetical calculation of probabilities involving contingent events, including further free human choices, that it is difficult to see how it could yield a secure basis for the constitution of a moral norm."[57]

McCormick had apparently realized before the appearance of Johnstone's article that the determining of counterproductivity was not necessarily a simple affair. In 1981 he put forward the tentative view that judgments of counterproductivity are "probably made in different ways depending on the issues at stake." Experience, he says, has shown us that certain actions are counterproductive. In other cases we have such a strong sense of revulsion "that we are grateful that we have not as yet had the experience." In a third category of cases we just have to proceed by trial and error.[58]

Johnstone, however, found another difficulty in all this talk about counterproductivity. He did not see why undermining a value in a generalized sense was disproportionate and therefore constitutive of moral wrongness while a particular negation of a value, as, for example, the direct killing of an innocent person, was not. He asked why the generalization of the assault on the value was the decisive factor.[59]

If we couple Johnstone's difficulties with the arguments advanced by Schüller, we are certainly left with the impression that something is missing in all this talk about counterproductivity if we are to understand that it is the most reliable, or perhaps even the only, indicator of disproportion. If, then, what has been proposed about counterproductivity is not enough, it would seem that comparisons between values and disvalues must be made, and, if they must be made, some rules of preference would appear to be needed. Some work has been done in this area in the United States. However, perhaps the best list of such guidelines that the present author has seen comes from the pen of the German theologian, Rudolf Ginters, although he does not claim that his list is complete. As the work in which this list appears has never, to my knowledge, been translated into English, we cannot claim that it is a part of the American debate on proportionalism. However, a brief glance at Ginter's ideas may provide some illumination and help us to pursue our topic more thoroughly.

Ginters gives five rules for actions which have a productive character: (1) preference should be given to the higher value; (2) quantity must be taken into account as well as quality (e.g., we should implement the kind of rescue operation that will save the greatest number of lives); (3) the more fundamental values should be preferred (life, of course, being one of the most fundamental); (4) the action which has the better chance of success should be preferred; (5) we should protect the values which have most urgent need of protection.[60] Ginters also speaks about a distributive rule. The amount of good that each person can realize is limited. The number of people to whom that good can be extended is also limited. However, the problem should not be formulated as: "What should I do and for whom?", but rather as: "What should I do in the context of the coordinated activity of all, and for whom?" Thus the greater good of all emerges from the actions of all. For example, parents should care first for the interests of their own children, and then for those of other people's children; the fight against crime is principally the responsibility of the police and then of the ordinary citizen.[61]

In addition to the productive actions, there are others which Ginters calls "expressive" (while Schüller calls them "symbolic").[62] Many of our actions are of an expressive character, he says, citing numerous examples, including praising, blaspheming, smiling and protesting.[63] Here too he refers to rules of preference similar to those applicable in the case of productive actions. For example, even in expressive actions, greater attention should be given to the higher value. This rule is broken, he says, if people show more indignation when an animal is harmed than they do when a man is harmed.[64]

Ginters' list may seem very complicated to some people, and, indeed, it is this very problem of an apparently complicated calculation which is at the center of one of Connery's main objections to proportionalism. He feels that proportionalism "makes moral decision making more difficult than is healthy for moral life." He sees being imposed upon the person a kind of calculation that makes moral assessment "largely inaccessible, if not impossible."[65] An even more radical objection, however, endeavors to show that any attempt at establishing rules of preference is futile. It is an objection based on the same impossibility that Knauer introduced right at the beginning of the debate. Knauer himself, we have seen, tried to overcome the problem by having recourse to counterproductivity as the determinant of moral wrongfulness (and even badness). We have also seen, however, that there are weaknesses in his arguments about counterproductivity. So what is to be said about his "impossibility" and consequent claims regarding the futility of trying to establish rules of preference? Paul Ramsey writes that, during our pilgrimage toward the greatest good, we may come across many goods claiming our allegiance which are not measurable.[66] Values, he says, may be comparable qualitatively, but we have no way of measuring an increase in one against a diminution of another.[67] Further on in the same article he suggests "that Schüller has ignored the incommensurability that is actually constitutive of some sorts of choices among nonmoral goods and evils to which we are sensitised by the identification of evil done only with indirect voluntariety."[68]

Germain Grisez is much more scathing. He describes proportionalism as "rationally unworkable." Its proponents, he says, do not tell us how to measure harms or benefits, and yet these must be commensurable if we are to make any kind of reasonable judgment about which is the lesser evil. "Although proportionalists are aware of this problem, none has solved it or even offered the plausible beginning of a solution."[69] In short, the proportionalists have no method for measuring harms and benefits.[70] Grisez himself sees our purposes, or the goods we seek, in eight categories. These are: life, play, aesthetic experience, speculative knowledge, integrity, practical reasonableness, friendship and religion. Regarding the first four, Grisez says that they can be understood

> without reference to the action of an agent seeking to realise them. As purposes, their meaning is independent of human action (which is not to say that they themselves have an independent existence, as if they were Platonic Ideas, but only that the activity of someone trying to realise them is not included in what they mean).[71]

The latter four categories of goods can also be sought for their own sake, but their meaning, says Grisez, inherently implies human action. "Self determining action is involved in their very meaning."[72] He calls the first four "substantive" purposes and the second four "reflexive" purposes. In answer to the possible objection that there may be more than eight categories, Grisez replies that, if we examine other purposes, we find that they are no more than "aspects or combinations of aspects of these fundamental goods."[73] Patriotism, for example, "is no more than a limited aspect of the broader category of goods we have called 'friendship'."[74] Whenever we make a choice, he maintains, the object of the choice is in some way one of these basic goods.

One thing that complicates choosing is the fact that these goods are not reducible to one another and do not have a common denominator. There is no objective hierarchy of values among these eight fundamental goods "because each in its own way is most important."[75] Grisez spells out this point:

> Life is most important because unless people live they lose the opportunity to realise any other purposes. Speculative knowledge is most important because unless people have a grasp of truth they live truncated, partial lives. Religion is most important because unless people are on satisfactory terms with God (the transcendent) nothing else really matters. And so on. Looked at from its own point of view, each fundamental purpose is most important.[76]

At this stage, it would be useful to clarify one or two things regarding

Grisez's complaint about method. A careful examination of the writings of the proportionalists reveals that they do not in fact propose a method. A few guidelines do not constitute a method. In a world in which methodology was canonized long ago, its absence could be disturbing to some people. However, there are times when we do well to confess our ignorance, even about the way we do everyday things, and that, I think, is what proportionalists in general do. Much of what we do lacks method in the sense that we do it without working out any precise methodology, and yet we do it very efficiently.

As long as Grisez and others continue to insist on the need for a well-defined method and continue to insist upon the incommensurability of values, certain aspects of this debate, it would seem, must remain unresolved. The present writer would therefore beg Grisez to look at his own way of resolving moral dilemmas. He insists that life and friendship are incommensurable. However, if he were presented with the choice between upsetting a friend to the point of losing his friendship and allowing somebody to die, would he really *need* to work out a method before making his choice? I should be insulting a highly respected philosopher if I were to suggest that he did.

Granted, then, this lack of method, which appears to be inevitable, we must now ask whether the proportionalists have been able to shed any light on the problem of incommensurability. In the case of legitimate self-defense a man may use as much violence as necessary to defend himself, even going so far as to kill his assailant. If there are two, three or more assailants, he may kill all of them, if necessary. This is a case of one life against several, and yet we say that he is right to choose to save the one and dispose of the others. Obviously, something other than numbers is being estimated. That is not really surprising. Human beings, suggests Vacek, are not mere computers which can handle only data reducible to multiples of a common denominator. They function more complexly than that.[77] In saying that, he is answering Grisez and Boyle, who argue that proportionalism is a calculative method and that such calculations cannot be made because the values cannot be measured against each other without a common denominator.[78] He goes on to point out that, although value is not a quantifiable standard, it does allow for comparisons. If that were not so, it would be impossible to claim that human beings are more valuable than stones.[79]

In a very recent article, the Irish theologian Bartholomew Kiely writes that each consequence of an act must in its turn be judged in connection with the further consequences that it causes, occasions or prevents. This process, he says, goes on into infinity. It is therefore impossible for us to know all the consequences of any given act. "Therefore the information on which a complete proportionalist assessment should be based cannot be attained."[80] Now, it is certainly true that we cannot accurately predict all the consequences of our actions, but it does not follow from this that those consequences which are predictable are not to be taken into account in our judgments about the rightness or wrongness of actions. Over the centuries the norm forbidding false statements was gradually whittled down to make room for equivocations, ambiguous statements, and eventually even occasional downright untruths. Surely, Kiely would admit that this process was necessitated by awareness of the predictably disastrous consequences that spring from truth-telling in certain situations. In the article under discussion he does in fact concede that "responsible action involves taking account of such consequences as are probable." However, he says, our usual way of linking acts with their consequences is deductive. We just assume that "intelligibly good acts" will have good consequences, while "intelligibly bad acts" will have bad consequences. "In other words, we attempt to see what the proper consequences of an act will be."[81] Now, what does Kiely mean by "intelligibly good/bad acts"? Is telling the truth intelligibly good? Suppose I am a university professor in a totalitarian state. I am sympathetic toward the activities of a certain rebel who is one of my students. One day a member of the secret police comes to the university. I am a well-respected citizen and he has no reason to suspect that I am sympathetic to the rebel cause. So, he trustingly asks me if I have seen "x" (the student rebel) in the university today. Am I to indulge in the "intelligibly good act" of telling the truth, even though I know that the immediate result of such a course of action would be a ring of steel around the university, the arrest of "x" and his subsequent execution? Kiely might say that the act of telling the truth in such circumstances is obviously intelligibly bad. However, he can only do so if he takes the predictable or probable consequences into account.

At this point he might complain that he is being grossly misinterpreted. He does admit, after all, that responsible action involves taking probable consequences into account. What he is saying is that "ordinarily we follow the deductive line." He gives the example of breaking a promise. We just assume, he says, that it will lead to resentment, the breakdown of trust, etc.[82] That may well be true. But is it an argument against proportionalism? Does any proportionalist say that we do *not* ordinarily follow the deductive line? Breaking a promise is surely recognized as an evil (a premoral one) by all proportionalists. So is telling an untruth. Most proportionalists, I am sure, would say that, in most cases, one judges, without getting involved in any conscious calculations, that it is wrong to tell an untruth or break a promise. We know immediately in most cases that there is no proportionate reason for bringing about the bad consequences of resentment, a breakdown of trust, etc. However, in some cases, there is such a proportionate reason, as is the case in the example given above, and we only know that by foreseeing the evil consequences of telling the truth, keeping a promise, etc., and "weighing" them against the premoral goods which could be achieved.

(c) *Are Deontological Norms Needed for Questions of Justice?*   Even if we accept, however, that proportionalism is possible, the possibility of its universal application is another matter. Do some acts lie outside its "calculations" for reasons other than the apparent incommensurability of goods and nongoods? The reader will recall W.D. Ross's objections to utilitarianism. There are duties, it seemed to him, which cannot be grounded on productivity of the greatest good, an example being promise keeping. Moreover, he pointed out, the duty to do what is just does not refer to production of the greatest good, but to the right distribution of it. Similar objections have been made in the United States by opponents of proportionalism.

> Since McCormick may yet be what we outsiders call a utilitarian of some sort, it should be pointed out, as was intimated earlier, that deontologists have advanced some objections to all forms of utilitarianism. Like many others, I myself have contended that a principle of justice is needed for an adequate morality *in addition* to any principle of utility (or love, for that matter).[83]

Other authors, including Connery, have spoken of problems of justice as if they were unresolvable within the confines of proportionalism.[84] One example of a justice problem which appears again and again in the debate on proportionalism and has been thought by some to be damning for the proportionalist case is taken from Anglo-Saxon philosophy. It concerns a rape case in a southern town in the United States. The mob is rioting and is threatening to kill a number of innocent people unless the culprit is brought to justice. The sheriff could avoid the need for a long search and save the lives of the people who would be killed by the mob if he framed a black man whom he knows to be innocent. The black man would be executed, but a number of others would be saved. Would a proportionalist be forced by his own way of arguing to accept such a solution? Schüller thinks not. He points out that the whole institution of criminal law is at stake here.[85] That may be true, but the present writer finds himself asking if Schüller is not searching for extra premoral evils which are not really necessary. Is the act not wrong even without taking the institution of criminal law into account? Hallett suggests we place ourselves in the imaginary sheriff's situation and assume that no refined calculations have entered his head. He simply wants to avoid a mass lynching and therefore decides to sacrifice a man he knows to be innocent. What, asks Hallett, do we think of that? If his reasoning and conclusions are not acceptable to us, that does not mean that the teleological approach is inadequate in this and similar cases. "For those who spontaneously rule against framing the prisoner do so because the death or suffering of an innocent man carries more weight with them than does the likelihood that others will die."[86]

It would seem, therefore, that those who spontaneously rule against the framing of the innocent man do not find it necessary to widen the net and look for more premoral evils. They see that the premoral evil in the act already outweighs any premoral good that could come from it. In other words, they already see that there is no proportionate reason for the act. Now let us take a look at a somewhat different situation:

> The example of fairness is that of a person who wants a certain candidate elected. He knows that the vast majority of his fellow citizens feel the same way and will vote for this candidate; so he himself stays home.[87]

Here it could seem to some who are seeking a utilitarian solution that the consequences establish the act as morally right. We have seen, however, that proportionalists are not concerned merely with such consequences and efficiency. In this case, for example, as Schüller points out, there is a lack of an expression of solidarity.[88] We have already seen what he and Ginters have to say on the subject of symbolic or expressive actions. They too involve premoral goods and premoral evils, and premoral evils must be kept to a minimum.[89] We can therefore resolve the problem of promise breaking. Breaking a promise is itself a premoral evil, and may be a very serious one. That, then, must enter into our "calculations." If, for example, I promise my friend that I will give five hundred dollars to his mother, and then contemplate giving the money to a charitable organization where it will be more useful, proportionalism does not permit me merely to balance the usefulness of the money in the two alternatives. I must also take into account the premoral evil involved in breaking the promise. As Cahill puts it:

> Some deontologists like Frankena would argue that equality must be premised on a principle of justice distinct from that of beneficence. However, if "doing good" is taken in the comprehensive teleological sense and not in the narrow utilitarian one, then considerations of fairness and respect for persons may also be included.[90]

3. Teleology, Deontology and Theological Tradition

A number of those who are opposed to proportionalism are generally referred to as "conservatives." The word "conservative" can, of course, give an impression of safety and orthodoxy. What is conserved is sometimes called "tradition" and that word is sometimes spelt with a capital "T" (although it is often little more than a synonym for "what some people began saying a long time ago," and "a long time ago" can be as little as a couple of centuries).[91] The so-called conservatives we are concerned with here, however, are also described as "deontologists," and yet, when Schüller took a look back over the centuries, he found that the tradition of the church was overwhelmingly teleological. Not surprising, he thought, for Christian ethics seeks to be an ethics of love, and "it seems scarcely comprehensible that the chief commandment of love could harmonize with any deontological norm."[92] How, for example, could love demand that we let an innocent man fall into the hands of his cruel enemy rather than protect him by telling an untruth? Naturally, Schüller admits the existence of deontological norms in traditional Catholic moral theology, but he points out that they constitute a small segment of all the ethical norms of behavior which have been handed down to us. Moreover, the problematic nature of these deontological norms was sensed by moral theologians of earlier generations who therefore restricted them as far as possible in favor of teleological considerations. For example, the concept of the false statement was restricted so as not to include double-meaning assertions, the aim of this and similar restrictions apparently being "to minimize the instances in which the fulfilment of deontological norms results in disproportionate harm to an individual or society."[93]

A few years ago Janssens produced an article dedicated to the question of proportionality in the writings of St. Thomas. If we have to pass a verdict on another person's act, he says, we first consider the exterior action and its object (what is done), take into account "all the observable circumstances and the perceptible elements of the situation," and try to discover the agent's motives and end. Janssens calls this the juridical approach and notes that it is the only one possible for an outsider because we cannot have direct insight into the interior act of someone else's will. In his moral approach, continues Janssens, Thomas dissociates himself from this juridical procedure. He takes as his starting point the inner act of the will and its proper object, which can be called the end. It is this end, in Janssens' reading of St. Thomas, which confers the moral species on an act. He then goes on to say that, in Aquinas' scheme of things, "what we do has to be proportioned to the end in the sense that it must be able to be really *id quod est ad finem,* an effective means to the end."[94]

William E. May, however, is of the opinion that, if we examine the teaching of St. Thomas on the structure and the moral meaning of human acts, we find that "for him it is possible, indeed necessary, to make a moral judgment about the exterior act as specified by its object without relating this to the end that the agent has in view in choosing the external act as a means." Thomas, he goes on to say, supported the thesis "that certain kinds of actions specified by their objects and describable in non-moral language (e.g., to have coition with someone who is not one's spouse . . .) are of themselves (*secundum se*) morally wicked and can never be justified by relating them to any end, however noble, that the agent may intend." In spite of Janssens' attempts to make him say so, continues May, Aquinas never taught that a person could do ontic evil for the sake of a greater ontic good.[95]

It is often interesting to see how opposing scholars find Aquinas going in two directions at the same time. It may well be that Thomas was of the opinion "that certain kinds of actions specified by their objects and describable in nonmoral language" are always morally wrong. Perhaps uttering a falsehood knowingly would be a good example. However, as Janssens points out in an earlier article, had Thomas taken into account the totality of human speech, thus recognizing it as a social phenomenon, he might have seen the necessity of using it sometimes to conceal the truth about something for the good of social relations.[96] The important point, moreover, is not that Thomas or any other theologian who lived a long time ago had up his sleeve a few exceptions to the teleological approach. It is rather that, like the whole Catholic tradition, his approach was overwhelmingly teleological. On the subject of uttering falsehoods (and probably some other items), the proportionalists do not appear to be in agreement with St. Thomas. That, however, does not indicate a break with tradition, although it could mean (and in the case of the uttering of falsehoods does appear to mean) that here and there St. Thomas made mistakes.[97]

4. Conclusions

That proportionalism is a teleological theory in the general run of Catholic theological tradition seems to be beyond dispute. However, we have seen that the word "teleological," like so many other words in this debate ("good," "bad," "direct," "indirect," "intention," etc.) can be misleading. In the proportionalist calculation, the τελοζ aimed at is not the only one to be taken into account. The foreseeable consequences not aimed at must also be included, although the τελοζ aimed at will, of course, be the reason for the act. The word "consequences" must also be added to our list of ambiguous and misleading terms. Perhaps it is even a bad choice, for, in proportionalism, we must take into account not only the consequences properly so called, but also dignity values, expressive actions, institutional obligations, the very meaning of the action, etc.

The problem of calculating proportion (in spite of the fact that such calculation is part of "tradition") has been exaggerated to the point of being described as impossible by writers on both sides of the debate. Vacek would appear to be right in pointing out that what is impossible for computers is not necessarily impossible for the creature created in the image and likeness of God. Difficulties (even great difficulties) there most certainly are, and perhaps lists of rules of preference like that prepared by Ginters can be of some assistance.

As for justice, fairness and promise-keeping problems, they are already overcome by what we have said regarding the misnomer "consequences": such elements as the unfairness of a situation or the breaking of a promise must most certainly be taken into account in the proportionalist calculation. Did somebody suggest that they should not? No, but perhaps proportionalists were a little late in stating clearly that such elements form part of the proportionalist calculation.

Notes

1. P. Foot, Introduction to *Theories of Ethics*, ed. P. Foot (Oxford, 1967), 1.
2. J. Kovesi, "*Principia Ethica* Re-examined: The Ethics of a Proto-logical Atomism,"

Philosophy 59 (1984): 157. He adds in a footnote: "Hume himself has equally been appropriated by contemporary British moral philosophy. But however inaccurately the tag 'Hume on "is" and "ought" ' is used, it does identify the tradition that uses this tag." Ibid., footnote 1.

3. W.K. Frankena, "The Naturalistic Fallacy," in *Theories of Ethics*, 53.

4. The fundamental quality Good was usually printed with a capital "G" in Moore's works.

5. G.E. Moore, "Is Goodness a Quality?," in *Aristotelian Society Proceedings, Supp. Vol. 11,* (London, 1932), 127.

6. C. Lewy, "G.E. Moore on the Naturalistic Fallacy," in *G.E. Moore Essays in Retrospect,* ed. A. Ambrose and M. Lazerowitz (London, 1970), 292–303. Moore had expressed a wish that, after his death, Lewy should go through his philosophical papers and consider the possibility of preparing a selection of them for publication. See G.E. Moore, *The Commonplace Book 1919–1953,* ed. C. Lewy (London, 1962), vii.

7. C. Lewy, "G.E. Moore on the Naturalistic Fallacy," 293.

8. Ibid., 295.

9. Ibid.

10. Referring to ethical theories which involve the so-called naturalistic fallacy, R.M. Hare describes "naturalist" as "an unfortunate term, for as Moore says himself, substantially the same fallacy may be committed by choosing metaphysical or suprasensible character- istics for this purpose. Talking about the supernatural is no prophylactic against 'natu- ralism'." R.M. Hare, *The Language of Morals* (Oxford, 1952), 82. Frankena says: "Mr. Moore should have added that, when one confuses 'good,' which is not a metaphysical object or quality, with any metaphysical object or quality, as metaphysical moralists do, according to him, then the fallacy should be called the metaphysical fallacy" (W.K. Frankena, "The Naturalistic Fallacy," 56).

11. C. Lewy, art. cit., 297.

12. Ibid.

13. P. Foot, op. cit., 2.

14. Ibid.

15. G.E. Moore, *Ethics* (London, 1958), 143. Moore's emphasis is reminiscent of Knauer's oft repeated "auf die Dauer und im ganzen" in his 1981 article.

16. J.P. Hill, *The Ethics of G.E. Moore: A New Interpretation* (Assen, 1976), 122.

17. C.D. Broad, *Five Types of Ethical Theory* (London, 1930), 206–07.

18. G.E. Moore, *Ethics,* 121 (emphasis his).

19. W.D. Ross, *Foundations of Ethics* (Oxford, 1939), 6–7. When he wrote this book, Ross took into account the reactions of other scholars to his earlier work, *The Right and the Good* (published in 1930).

20. Ibid., 42. The reader will recall our brief discussion about Hume, Moore, "ought from is" and the naturalistic fallacy. Having described naturalistic theories as those which "hold that ethical characteristics can be analysed without remainder into non-ethical ones," C.D. Broad notes that Hume held a naturalistic view. C.D. Broad, op. cit., 257–58.

21. Ibid., 316.

22. Ibid., 320.

23. Ibid., 320–21. The emphasis on "seems" in the last sentence is his. I have heard people misrepresent Ross by saying that, according to him, when we are faced with a choice between *prima facie* duties, we simply see or know which of them is our real duty.

24. See P. Hughes, *The Reformation in England* (London 1954), 344, footnote 2.

25. For more detail on this point, see J.F. Dedek's articles listed in footnote 87 of Chapter One. Dedek is of the opinion that later theologians were generally unwilling to oppose the authority of Augustine ("Moral Absolutes. . . ," 680). See also L.I. Ugorji, *The Principle of Double Effect. A Critical Appraisal of Its Traditional Understanding and Its Modern Interpretation* (Frankfurt, 1985), 84–85.

26. During this period, it seems, neither Catholics nor Protestants would have smiled on the telling of untruths with the intention of deceiving in the circumstances described above. As it was, the Catholics met with some Protestant criticism regarding their use of ambiguous statements or mental reservations when answering the questions of government agents. Mental reservation also had something of a stormy ride within the Catholic Church itself, but eventually became generally accepted in some forms when there was a good enough reason for concealing the truth. Interestingly, however, Dedek notes that the distinction between a false statement and a lie was "already foreshadowed in the writings of Peter of Poitiers and St. Albert the Great, but it never took hold or was developed in the medieval tradition" (J.F. Dedek, "Intrinsically Evil Acts. . . ," 412).

27. W.D. Ross, *Foundations of Ethics,* 319.

28. W.D. Ross, "The Meaning of 'Good'," in *Travaux du IXe Congrès International de Philosophie,* Vol. XI, Part II (Paris, 1937), 79.

29. O.A. Johnson, *Rightness and Goodness* (The Hague, 1959), 158.

30. I say "most" having in mind G.E.M. Anscombe, who appears to be much closer than Ross to the species of deontologist found in Catholic moral theology circles.

31. R.A. McCormick, *Notes . . . 1965 through 1980,* 353.

32. J.R. Connery, "Morality of Consequences. . . ," 248.

33. R.A. McCormick, *Notes . . . 1965 through 1980,* 685. See F. Böckle, "Glaube und Handeln," *Concilium* 120 (1976): 644.

34. Ibid., 717.

35. Ibid., 762.

36. Ibid., footnote 41.

37. Earlier in the same article he refers to Gustav Ermecke's misunderstanding Fuchs in this way (ibid., 531). See G. Ermecke, "Das Problem der Universalität oder Allgemeingültigkeit sittlicher Normen innerweltlicher Lebensgestaltung," *Münchener Theologische Zeitschrift* 24 (1973): 1–24, and Fuchs's reply: "Sittliche Normen—Universalien und Generalisierungen," *Münchener Theologische Zeitschrift* 25 (1974): 18–33.

38. R.A. McCormick, *Notes . . . 1965 through 1980,* 541.

39. J.R. Connery, "Catholic Ethics: Has the Norm for Rule-Making Changed?," *Theological Studies* 42 (1981): 234, footnote 4.

40. Ibid., footnote 5.

41. Ibid., 246.

42. R.A. McCormick, *Notes . . . 1981 through 1984,* 63.

43. Fuchs has referred to this fuller sense of "object" in his writings. He gives the example of the removal of a kidney—from a healthy man—to perform a transplant on another man who needs a kidney. All of this (the object in the narrow sense, the circumstances, and the end) constitutes the object in the full sense. See J. Fuchs, *Essere del Signore* (Rome, 1981), 196.

44. J.R. Connery, "The Teleology of Proportionate Reason," *Theological Studies* 44 (1983): 490.

45. L.S. Cahill, "Teleology, Utilitarianism and Christian Ethics," 603.

46. Ibid., 627.

47. See footnote 17.

48. J. Seifert, "Absolute Moral Obligations towards Finite Goods as Foundations of Intrinsically Right and Wrong Actions," *Anthropos* 1 (Rome 1985): 67.

49. Ibid., 67–68.

50. P. Knauer, "The Hermeneutic Function. . . ," 11.

51. Ibid., 14.

52. B. Schüller, "Neuere Beiträge. . . ," 163–64.

53. "Das ist gewissermassen eine Minderung des Wertes selbst" (P. Knauer, "Fundamentalethik. . . ," 337).

54. A. Koestler, *The Roots of Coincidence* (London, 1972), 101.

55. R.A. McCormick, *Ambiguity in Moral Choice* (Milwaukee: Marquette University, 1973), 94.

56. McCormick's views on the direct/indirect distinction will be examined in greater detail in Chapter Five.

57. B.V. Johnstone, "The Meaning of Proportionate Reason in Contemporary Moral Theology," *The Thomist* 49 (1985): 246–47.

58. R.A. McCormick, *Notes . . . 1981 through 1984*, 16.

59. B.V. Johnstone, art. cit., 247.

60. R. Ginters, *Werte und Normen: Einführung in die Philosophische und Theologische Ethik* (Düsseldorf, 1982), 215–16.

61. Ibid., 216.

62. B. Schüller, "Various Types of Grounding for Ethical Norms," in *Readings . . . No. 1*, 194–96.

63. R. Ginters, op. cit., 92–94.

64. Ibid., 216.

65. J.R. Connery, "Catholic Ethics: Has the Norm for Rule-Making Changed?," 250. See also "The Teleology of Proportionate Reason," *Theological Studies* 44 (1983): 494.

66. P. Ramsey, "Incommensurability and Indeterminacy in Moral Choice," in *Doing Evil to Achieve Good*, 70.

67. Ibid., 71.

68. Ibid., 75.

69. G. Grisez, *The Way of the Lord Jesus*, Vol. 1, *Christian Moral Principles* (Chicago, 1983), 152.

70. Ibid.

71. G. Grisez and R. Shaw, *Beyond the New Morality*, 71.

72. Ibid.

73. Ibid., 73.

74. Ibid.

75. Ibid., 75.

76. Ibid., 76.

77. E. Vacek, "Proportionalism: One View of the Debate," *Theological Studies* 46 (1985): 304.

78. See G. Grisez and J. Boyle, Jr., *Life and Death with Liberty and Justice* (Notre Dame, Ind.: University of Notre Dame, 1979).

79. E. Vacek, art. cit., 304.

80. B.M. Kiely, "The Impracticality of Proportionalism," *Gregorianum* 66 (1985): 661–63.
81. Ibid., 664.
82. Ibid., 665.
83. W.K. Frankena, "McCormick and the Traditional Distinction," 161–62.
84. See J.R. Connery, "Morality of Consequences. . . ," 261.
85. B. Schüller, "The Double Effect in Catholic Thought. . . ," 177.
86. G. Hallett, *Christian Moral Reasoning: An Analytic Guide* (Notre Dame, Ind. 1983), 97.
87. R.A. McCormick, *Notes . . . 1965 through 1980,* 540. Here he is describing the discussion between Connery and Schüller on the point.
88. See Schüller's discussion with Connery in "Neuere Beiträge. . . ," 164–81, and "Various Types. . . ," 194–96.
89. One of the principal points made by proportionalists has been that "we have the moral obligation to reduce as much as possible the ontic evil which comes about when we act" (L. Janssens, "Ontic Evil and Moral Evil," 79).
90. L.S. Cahill, "Teleology, Utilitarianism and Christian Ethics," 629.
91. Even the principle of double effect, in the form in which it came down to us, would appear to be quite modern, and yet it is often referred to as "traditional."
92. B. Schüller, "Various Types. . . ," 186.
93. Ibid. The Italian theologian, Enrico Chiavacci, writes: "Nella morale cattolica ereditata da una lunga tradizione di Chiesa sussistono precetti di ambedue i tipi [teleological and deontological]; ma tutti debbono esser visti nella luce dell'unico comandamento che riassume e giustifica ogni precetto operativo: il comandamento della carità. La morale cristiana non può essere che una morale della chiamata. Anche un precetto deontologico ha in essa significato e funzione; la sua deduzione razionale indica che esso è un elemento—talora importantissimo come il 'non uccidere'—per scoprire la chiamata e darsi una norma corrispondente: ma non è mai l'elemento definitivo. Così la riflessione morale e l'eventuale formulazione di precetti potrà e dovrà seguire anche piste di tipo deontologico: lo abbiamo visto a proposito della legge naturale. Ma la norma morale dovrà sempre esser fondata teleologicamente" (E. Chiavacci, *Teologia Morale 1/Morale Generale* (Assisi, 1979), 229).
94. L. Janssens, "Saint Thomas Aquinas and the Question of Proportionality," *Louvain Studies* 9 (1982): 45.
95. W.E. May, "Aquinas and Janssens on the Moral Meaning of Human Acts," *The Thomist* 48 (1984): 605.
96. L. Janssens, "Ontic Evil and Moral Evil," 73–78.
97. Thomas does seem to have applied a teleological approach even to the uttering of falsehoods. Janssens notes that, according to Aquinas, a priest may protect the secret of the confessional even by declaring under oath that he knows nothing, the confessor having this right for the following reason: "*qua* human being he does not know anything because he knows it only the way God knows it since he represents God" (ibid., 76). Surely, such verbal gymnastics were made necessary by Thomas' awareness of the fact that the priest has to find an effective means to the end (the protection of the confessional secret).

We have already had occasion to see how a certain amount of confusion has slipped into various aspects of the debate on proportionalism. The existence of widespread misunderstandings is therefore not at all surprising. Several are evident and in need of no comment at this stage in the following attack on the teleological approach by an author who obviously sees Catholic moral tradition as deontological: "As proposed by B. Schüller, K. Demmer and E. Chiavacci, *teleological ethics* should replace the traditional 'deontological ethics' in which the norms are deduced from general principles regardless of concrete conditions. According to this theory, all human deeds should be oriented 'teleologically' [In the article 'theologically' appears here, apparently a printing error], i.e., to the aim, the happiness of all concerned persons. This aim decides the moral value of all acts. Consequently, there are no human acts morally wrong in and of their own nature. For instance, contraception and sterilisation are morally good if they are used to implement reasonable family planning. However, neither aim of action nor concrete conditions have been neglected in the principles of traditional Christian ethics, though they could, of course, have been neglected by the people applying them. Introducing principles of teleological ethics would not rectify the Christian way of life; on the contrary, it would mean that the end justified the means. Such moral relativism is contrary to the foundations of Christian morality. As a matter of fact, teleological ethics is a new form of situation ethics, in disguise" (W.B. Skrzydlewski, "Conflict and Schism in Moral Theology and Sexual Ethics," *Homiletic and Pastoral Review* 85 (1985): 29).

CHAPTER FIVE

The Direct/Indirect Distinction

Both within and without the debate on proportionalism, it is not always clear what the subject is when mention is made of the direct/indirect distinction in morals. Before we go on to discuss the part it has played in our debate, a few words of introduction to the problem might not, therefore, be out of place.

What Knauer presented to the world in various articles between 1965 and 1981 was both a reduction and an extension. He reduced the requirements of the principle of double effect to the need for a proportionate reason, but he then sought to apply what he continued to call "the principle of double effect" right across the board. For him, "it is, in reality, the fundamental principle of all morality."[1] Until Knauer came on the scene, however, the principle of double effect led, as he himself admits, "a marginal existence in the handbooks of moral theology."[2] Although it is sometimes difficult to see the wood for the trees when reading about this principle, it would seem that, traditionally, it was applied to acts which had both good and bad effects, but the bad effects were understood to be intrinsically evil, in the sense that their *immediate* realization without the immediate realization of good effects was always morally wrong.[3] That does not, of course, mean that the production of such an evil was always wrong. The traditional understanding of the principle of double effect was that an act which would foreseeably cause such an evil as well as a good could be performed if, and only if, all four of the following conditions were fulfilled:

1. The act (directly) performed is in itself good, or at least indifferent.
2. The good accomplished is at least as immediate as the evil.
3. The intention of the agent is good.
4. There is a proportionate reason for causing the harm.[4]

In recent times there has been a tendency to dismiss the first condition on the grounds that it puts the cart before the horse. It is taken to mean that the act should not be morally wrong,[5] although the whole purpose of the principle is to help us decide whether acts with multiple effects are right or wrong. However, one sees a certain ingenuity in the formulation of the principle of double effect and is tempted to doubt that the mind or minds that produced it were capable of such blatant stupidity. Selling does not think that the people who originally formulated the principle intended by this first condition that the act should not be morally wrong. He thinks it is much more likely that the act should not contain *any* evil (even a premoral evil) from the very beginning. That would not mean that such an act could never be licit. It merely meant that the principle of double effect did not apply in that case. Some other principle (e.g., the principle of the lesser of two evils) should be used.[6] Selling continues:

> What I propose is that the principle of double effect applies, and is meant to apply, *only* to those cases where the doing of a good may result in a foreseeable evil. It must not be confused with cases where evil is done directly. One must consider why double effect is not applied to cases of capital punishment, imprisonment, disciplining children or civil or ecclesiastical censures, etc., and why it encounters so much difficulty when forced upon cases outside its competence, such as that of mutilation. The point is that anything that involves doing an evil directly—and the removal of a uterus regardless of the presence of a fetus is still an act of mutilation no matter how you slice it—we need another principle to deal with it morally.[7]

Be that as it may, the principle of double effect has frequently been applied in recent times—at least in theological writings—to cases which Selling describes (rightly, I think) as beyond its range. One of the more notable is perhaps the case of the therapeutic abortion. There the directness or indirectness of the killing came to be seen as having crucial importance. However, Selling says that the term "direct" does not have to appear in the principle of double effect, although "it often creeps in."[8] And, indeed, it would appear that the second condition of the principle requires only that the good effect should not proceed from the evil. The formulators were very likely concerned with the fact that the principle could only be used to justify acts with both good and evil *effects*. Actions which involved evils as *causes* could not be justified by the principle of double effect. Knauer would therefore appear to be changing things very radically by referring to aspects rather than effects. He may be right in thinking that

St. Thomas was really talking about aspects, but the principle of double effect which was passed on to us was not really expounded in that passage from the *Summa* quoted by Knauer.

What the formulators of the principle intended, however, and what was the usual interpretation when Knauer appeared on the scene, are not necessarily the same thing. Ugorji examines several formulations of the principle of double effect and concludes that the authors are referring to acts in which a *malum morale* is produced. They are also stating, he believes, that the act itself should not be morally wrong[9] and that the good effect may be *directly* intended by the agent while the evil effect must be only *indirectly* intended.[10] The principle of double effect, moreover, seems to have acquired a somewhat wider field of application than Selling would be inclined to grant it, even before Knauer's intervention. Indeed, Ugorji refers to the performance of a hysterectomy on a pregnant woman with a diseased uterus as "a classical application of the principle of double effect."[11] He concludes that the principle was designed to govern acts which produce both good and intrinsic evil simultaneously. "Its formulation rests on the belief that some values are '*per se*' intrinsically (morally) evil."[12] Ugorji may be wrong if he thinks that the original formulation was based on such a belief, but what was actually passed on to us from our forebears does seem to be based on that belief.

Knauer, moreover, would appear to be right in asserting that the direct/indirect distinction was held to be crucial. The evil had not to be directly intended. Now, in view of the fact that in traditional Catholic moral theology the intention was the reason for the act, one might feel inclined to scratch one's head and ask just what was meant by "directly intended." Selling points out that only the reason for the act is intended (in this sense of the verb "to intend"). Everything else in the act is unintended.[13] Perhaps some explanation is called for at this point. In modern language, "to intend" has another meaning. Let us suppose, by way of example, that an armed policeman comes upon a horrifying scene. A man is about to kill a child. Being too far away to intervene quickly enough in another way, the policeman pulls out his gun and shoots the man. Later, at the inquest into the man's death, the policeman is asked: "Did you *intend* to kill the man?" He replies: "I had no time to waste and could not afford to take chances. Yes, I *intended* to kill him." Clearly, his *reason* for killing the man was to save the child, but he did *intend* to kill the man. In the traditional language of moral theology, the evil of killing in this case would have been voluntary, but not intended.[14] There is, of course, no contradiction here. The word "intend" merely has two different meanings.

The evil in the act could therefore be intended in the psychological sense (i.e., the usual sense), but had not to be intended directly in the moral sense. What does that mean? It would be hazardous to suppose that all authorities (whatever *that* word means) would have given the same answer to that question. That much is clear from an exchange that occurred some years ago. In 1953, Gerard Kelly examined some of the writings of Fathers Hurth and McCarthy on the subject of direct killing. McCarthy, it seems, was of the opinion that a killing was direct when the immediate and *per se* object of the act or omission was the destruction of human life. If, however, the death occurred *per accidens* as a result of the presence of factors which lay outside the immediate object of the act, the killing was indirect. In the case of the removal of a cancerous uterus from a pregnant woman, the death of the inviable fetus was thus described as a *per accidens* effect of the operation. Fr. Hurth's ideas were somewhat different. He was of the opinion that an act could have two equally immediate and *per se* effects. Thus, in certain cases involving the killing of a human person, death would be just one of the immediate and *per se* effects. In such cases, the nature of the action did not suffice to indicate whether or not the killing was direct. It was necessary to know the *finis operantis*. That is, in a case where there are two or more equally immediate and *per se* effects, the direct effect is the one which the agent has chosen; the other effects which he or she merely tolerates are indirect. A direct killing *ex fine operis* would apparently occur only in those cases in which the destruction of life is the only immediate effect of the action.

Kelly preferred Hurth's interpretation and declared that he thought that the notion of direct effect was aptly expressed in English by the term 'by-product.' An effect is indirect when it is an unintentional by-product of an action, the agent intentionally aiming at the production of another effect. However, he points out, a by-product is not necessarily a *per accidens* effect. Buttermilk, for example, is not just a *per accidens* effect in the making of butter, although it does seem to be a by-product. Similarly, when a cancerous pregnant uterus is removed, the death of the inviable fetus would not seem to be a merely *per accidens* effect, although that death and the sterility which results from the operation are unavoidable by-products of the hysterectomy. They retain the character of indirectness "as long as they are genuinely not intended."[15]

Referring to what he called "Fr. Kelly's attractive analogy," McCarthy asked to what extent buttermilk is an *unintentional* by-product, and how true it is that it is merely tolerated.

And suppose the housewife really wanted and intentionally aimed at producing the buttermilk—it is an excellent drink—rather than the butter, does the production of the buttermilk then become the direct effect and butter the by-product?[16]

If we look beyond the fascination for buttermilk and dairymaids, we see from this exchange that there was already disagreement regarding the meaning of "directly intended in the moral sense" long before the debate on proportionalism got under way. It would seem, then, that, in the world that present-day proportionalists were born into, the direct/indirect distinction was generally held to be of enormous importance. The only problem seems to have been a certain amount of disagreement about exactly what that distinction was supposed to involve. Suppose, then, that we accept that "direct signifies the performance of an external act," whilst "indirect signifies anything which flows from the act (or the results of setting a series of events into motion)."[17] Now, in Selling's understanding of the principle of double effect (which is very likely the understanding of its originators), such direct performance of a premoral evil to produce a premoral good could not, it would seem, be justified by that principle, although it could perhaps be justified by another—in which case the directness or indirectness (in this sense) of the production of the evil would apparently be of little or no importance. Such thinking, however, would produce the very physical interpretation that Knauer complained about.

Suppose, then, that we abandon these physical definitions of "direct" and "indirect," and we talk instead about directly and indirectly intending, as Knauer does. He holds, it will be remembered, that if there is not a proportionate reason for the act, the evil produced becomes part of the intention. In other words, it is directly intended. Now, in view of the fact that the intention is the reason for the act, what Knauer says sounds odd if worded differently: if the reason for the act is not proportionate, the evil in the act becomes part of the reason. The reason for an act is, of course, always good. What Knauer evidently means is that, if that good is not in proportion to the evil produced, the act is a morally wrong one.

Why, then, did he not say just that? Perhaps because he was at least subconsciously influenced by something that influenced at a more conscious level other theologians who were just as dissatisfied with the implications of a physical interpretation of the direct/indirect distinction as he was. That something was the widespread belief that certain acts were intrinsically evil regardless of circumstances and finalities. I say that

Knauer could have been influenced by that belief no more than subconsciously because, in his writings, he opposed it. Perhaps his failure to distinguish clearly between moral goodness and moral rightness contributed to this state of affairs.

However, even if Knauer was not being coherent in maintaining the direct/indirect distinction, it is easy to understand why some such distinction was maintained by those who really did believe in the existence of acts (or effects) which could be described as intrinsically evil regardless of circumstances and finalities. Sometimes it seemed necessary to bring about such an evil because common sense dictated that, for instance, a medicine which could save a man's life should be given to him, even if the doctor knew that it would cause sterility. In that and in many similar cases there was a kind of escape clause. The agent could bring about the evil, and yet claim at the same time that, in a way, he or she had not brought it about. Suppose a doctor removed a cancerous uterus from a pregnant woman and somebody then asked him if he had killed an innocent person, he could perhaps reply: "Yes . . . in a manner of speaking" or "Well, I did kill the child, but only in an indirect sort of way."

In this last mentioned case one might feel tempted to explain what is meant by "indirect" by claiming that the fetus just happened to be in the womb when the operation became necessary. However, in some other cases, the same kind of reasoning cannot be applied. In the case of an ectopic pregnancy, for example, most theologians would probably now agree that shelling out the fetus is preferable to excising the fallopian tube with the fetus inside it. In such a case, the intention is said by a number of theologians to be indirect. That, of course, can lead to all manner of difficulties, misunderstandings and uncertainties regarding what is meant. However, we shall let this brief sketch of at least some of the reasons for the present confusion suffice. We shall, of course, return to the problem of the exact meaning of "directness" and "indirectness" later. In the meantime, we need to take a look at what appears to have emerged as the source of the problem in the first place: the concept of intrinsic evil.

1. Intrinsic Evil

The term "intrinsic evil" tends to be associated with documents emanating from the Holy See, and yet James Murtagh notes that the first pontiff to use that formulation in an encyclical was Pius XI, who, in

Casti Conubii, asserted that those who deliberately frustrated the natural power and purpose of the procreative functions during intercourse performed an act which was *"intrinsece inhonestum."* He also asserted that no reason could be advanced to make what is intrinsically against nature conformable to nature and morally good.[18] This last assertion was repeated by Pius XII, who declared that "no indication or need can change an intrinsically immoral action into a moral and lawful act."[19] Turning to the subject of masturbation as a means of obtaining semen for purposes of artificial insemination, the same pope described it as contrary to nature and therefore intrinsically evil.[20] Referring to those two statements by Pius XII, Murtagh notes that they reveal two strands of thought. One is that an act which is intrinsically evil is always such regardless of circumstances. The other is that an act which is intrinsically evil is contrary to nature.[21] Paul VI imitated his predecessors by stating that an intrinsically evil act cannot be right. The particular acts he referred to as intrinsically dishonest "impede," he wrote, "the *natural* effect of the marriage act."[22]

As for the manuals, all those examined by Murtagh contained the axiom *"bonum ex integra causa, malum ex quocumque defectu."* From this it follows that "a good intention will not make a bad object good."[23] However, notes Murtagh, a few (though *only* a few) manualists explained how that axiom was to be understood. Vermeersch, for example, points out that it must be understood to apply to an action that would be good in all its elements, i.e., simply good. The act is, of course, not simply good if one of its elements is defective. Although such an act is not simply good, however, it is not necessarily immoral, because it is possible to have evil circumstances which would not change the substantial goodness of the act. Nevertheless, notes Murtagh, it is not clear that the axiom was always understood in that way. An improper understanding of it may have contributed to the tendency to identify the moral object with the physical object and moral evil with physical evil.[24]

Murtagh adds that, although it would be a misrepresentation to say that the manuals always identified the moral object with physical activity, "there are indications that this happened occasionally." In theory, he writes, it was never intended, but it did sometimes happen in practice.

In summary, then, we can say that there is an ambiguous use of the moral object in the manuals, and this could lead to an understanding of an intrinsic evil act as an act which is evil independent of all circumstances and motivation of the agent, because, as we have seen, intrinsic evil is usually discussed in relationship to the moral object.[25]

Going on to discuss Knauer's assertion that the *finis operis* is the moral object, and that the *finis operis* must be what is intended, he says that such an understanding of the object leads to the conclusion that the expressions "intrinsic evil" and "moral evil" are synonymous.[26] Murtagh himself concludes that they are indeed synonymous.[27] Here, however, a little caution is called for. Knauer, we have seen, has not always been careful to distinguish what is morally evil from what is morally wrong. I assume (although I am by no means sure) that when he uses the expression "moral evil," Murtagh means "morally wrong." After all, not even a diehard deontologist should be found asserting that contraception and sterilization are always sinful, in the proper sense of that word.

What concerns us, therefore, is the claim that there is an inherent wrongness in the performance of certain acts. Although Knauer seems at times to have confused the two levels of moral goodness/badness and moral rightness/wrongness, it is, of course, possible to include the intention in the object while endeavoring to judge the rightness or wrongness of an act. Indeed, as Fuchs points out, the object of an action which is judged to be intrinsically evil is presumably always "not simply the physical reality of the act but also its consequences or finalities." Nevertheless, he continues, while it is true that moral theologians accept that the object can include consequences, finalities and certain circumstances, "they distinguish these circumstances from further circumstances not yet foreseen in the described object of the act." The result of this distinction is that "in whatever way one prefers to determine the object of a moral action, the fact that this action is judged because of its object as 'intrinsically evil' means that it can never be rendered morally right by any further circumstances, consequences and finalities."[28]

People who hold that certain acts are always morally wrong regardless of consequences, finalities and circumstances are, of course, generally described as deontologists. What we discussed in Chapter Four regarding deontology and teleology could perhaps be described as purely philosophical. All of the points raised by the various parties could have been raised in a debate outside the church. However, the deontological norms that are to be found in the Catholic Church, and, therefore, the doctrine of intrinsic evil as it is generally understood, appear to be backed by a particular vision of God (not shared by the proportionalists) and a particular concept of the power that Jesus invested in his church.

Acts described as intrinsically evil regardless of additional circumstances, consequences and finalities are usually so described by Catholic deontologists on the grounds that they have the characteristic either of being contrary to nature—God's will presumably being expressed in the laws of nature—or of arrogating a right reserved to God. Human organs and faculties are seen as having natural ends. However, the natural ends of only a very few organs and faculties tend to be of interest to the deontologist. No attempt seems to be made to take on the (admittedly formidable) job of defining the natural ends of the hand, the brain, or that mysterious organ which seems so much an extra that it is summarily dismissed in common language as "the appendix," and tends to be known only for the acute pain which its inflammation sometimes causes. In general, we may say that the faculty of speech[29] and the genital organs are those which most interest the Catholic deontologist.

> Thus, for example, God gave speech to humans so that they might live together in community through truthful talk. Untruthful talk frustrates this divinely appointed goal and is therefore impermissible. This conviction is at bottom teleological in its presentation. It ends up in deontological norms only because its proponents appeal to the supreme wisdom of God in order to show that a natural end is unassailable. The speech of human beings must be truthful even though this may bring serious harm to another.[30]

Some premoral values are thus raised to the level of what Schüller calls "absolute preferability." According to the deontologists, they must always be preferred to any other competing value(s).

> In this way the integrity of certain biological laws can be a value to be preferred absolutely. This approach is thoroughly a-teleological in its consequences. For example, tradition maintains that the use of artificial contraceptives *as such* is impermissible; on the other hand, it judges that the Knaus-Ogino (rhythm) method is ethically permissible."[31]

Against this way of thinking, Schüller points out that we are justified in seeing the wisdom of God at work in certain natural ends which we judge to be "true and applicable," but, in individual cases, they must be weighed against other competing values. The making of the judgment in such a case "is the natural end of the capacity for judgment given to human beings by God."[32] As for the second type of argument, the usual example of an arrogation of a right reserved to God is self-killing. Only God, it is argued, is Lord of life and death. Any person who kills him- or herself is, according to this way of thinking, usurping a right reserved to God. Schüller points out that those who say this are begging the question.

From a theological standpoint the precise question is whether God does or does not exercise his mastery over the life of a human being in such a way that, through the ethical demands of given situations, he thereby empowers the human being to put an end to his own life.[33]

Those who hold that God's moral will is expressed in biological laws and that George may not kill himself unless God says to him: "George, you may kill yourself," obviously have a more anthropomorphic vision of God than Schüller, Fuchs, and, one imagines, just about any other proportionalist. In a recently published article,[34] Fuchs refers to some of the problems that can arise from such an excessively anthropomorphic vision of God (while admitting that all our utterances on the subject are inevitably anthropomorphic and symbolic). Some people in the church, he notes, go beyond the teaching that the value of norms and moral judgments is founded ultimately on God. They teach that innumerable concrete normative statements, products of human intelligence, are precepts or laws of God. Christians thus see themselves and their realization of man in the world compared with divine precepts. God seems to be the competitor that Nietzsche thought he saw in the minds of many Christians. This God, moreover, is pictured as watching over his global precepts in an unmoving way, not bothering to take real human differences into account. He is seen not so much as the God in whom we live and move and have our being, who rules over our existence as the ultimate foundation of our life and action, but more as the God who is alongside us in our categorial world, and who makes demands on us. From the moral point of view, he merely requires obedience.[35] However, says Fuchs, man is created to be lord of himself, while God's lordship is transcendent. It is incorrect to picture man merely as administrator of what the divine Sovereignty owns, and it is therefore equally incorrect, he says, to speak about divine authorization or delegation with regard to such matters as the disposing of human life. True human earthly authority is such, he says, not because God gives a legal character to man's "authoritative" arrangements, but because it is "created participation in the transcendent authority of God." Our search for and discovery of right behavior in this world have the character of moral norms because God has made man lord of the earth. This is true also with regard to very detailed judgments.[36]
It would, of course, be a gross exaggeration, and indeed somewhat offensive, to accuse the opponents of proportionalism of envisaging God writing his rules on the side of a mountain with bolts of lightning. The vision of God as legislator does, however, appear to play a major role in

the arguments of some of them. We have already had reason to note that one of the most influential members of the antiproportionalism camp is Germain Grisez. In his vision, God's legislation is not written on a mountainside, but it is written just as clearly in documents published by the Holy See. There are limits, he says, to the trust we can place in a moral guide who is merely human, and, if we surpass those limits, we act irresponsibly.

> But we believe that our Lord teaches in and through the Church and gives us the word of the Father. Hence, our submission to the Church's teaching is not submission to mere human opinions, but to the very word of God.[37]

We are no more intellectually irresponsible, he goes on to say, if we submit unreservedly to what the church teaches in the moral sphere than we are when we submit unreservedly to those fundamental doctrines that go beyond reason and experience, such as the Trinity, the Incarnation, etc.[38] But what is involved in following or submitting to the teachings and judgments of the church? As far as her members are concerned, the Catholic Church, says Grisez, "is the supreme moral authority under God." They must conform their consciences to what that church teaches "in every question, every detail, every respect." Those who are faithful will do so, not just because they hear the voice of Jesus in that teaching, "but because by their conscientious commitment of faith they have accepted the Church as their own, more than humanly wise, moral guide."[39]

What work is there for the conscience in this scheme of things? Well, according to Grisez, if I make the judgment of conscience that I should listen to a certain moral guide and follow whatever advice is given, then I go against my conscience if I listen to the advice of that guide and do not act accordingly. However, he adds, the conscience has more work than this to do. I have to make the church's teaching my own, and this work of appropriation is the work of my conscience. I must also add to the church's teaching whatever is compatible with it and necessary for the fulfillment of my personal vocation. If I have difficulties, I should make them known to my bishop. The bishop, in his turn, should examine such difficulties and provide guidance and help.[40]

Later in the same work, Grisez examines some examples of alleged errors in Catholic teaching. With regard to the Galileo case, he admits that the ordinary magisterium erred.

However, nothing in the historical record shows that the bishops scattered about the world taught (or that many of them ever thought about) the proposition Paul V mistakenly taught. And Paul V's teaching certainly was not *ex cathedra*. The Galileo case is an example of a situation in which the magisterium must teach firmly on a new question and can make a mistake.[41]

In the second draft of the original manuscript which was prepared primarily for theological students at Mount St. Mary's Seminary, Grisez added the words: "Until the teaching of the Church as a whole develops by the involvement of the whole *collegium* or by a papal definition, official teaching in the Church must be obeyed—which, in general, Galileo did." This sentence does not appear in the published work. Rightly so, I believe, but one wonders why Grisez removed it because elsewhere in the same book he says something very similar:

To fulfill their duty, bishops must venture to teach what has never been taught before, and sometimes they must propose this teaching as truth to be held definitively. In such cases, their teaching is official teaching within the Church and the faithful must accept it.

Nevertheless, in cases of this sort, bishops (including the pope) do not individually enjoy the gift of infallibly discerning what belongs to divine truth and what does not. Mistakes are possible. There is room for disagreement among bishops. Until the magisterium as a whole has spoken, one cannot be certain that such disagreement will not arise nor how it will be resolved. But until it is resolved the faithful must accept the teaching of the pope, or lacking such a teaching, that of their own bishop.[42]

It would seem, then, that Grisez advocates obedience to the pope or bishop even when the pope or bishop is wrong. If we carry that to its logical conclusion, we find that, according to Grisez, a person should conform with official teaching even when his or her conscience dictates otherwise. I am sure that Grisez would be appalled to find himself being accused of teaching people to act against their consciences, but how can he counter such an accusation? He appears, moreover, to go so far as to envisage God either making mistakes or misleading people:

One who makes the act of human faith—that is, accepts teaching with religious assent even when it is not recognisable as infallibly proposed—can proceed with confidence and a clear conscience. If the teaching should turn out to be in error, one has nevertheless followed the guidance which God has seen fit to provide.[43]

2. The Importance of the Direct/Indirect Distinction for Some Opponents of Proportionalism

Between them, Schüller and Fuchs would appear to have dealt something of a death blow to the traditional understanding of *intrinsece malum*[44] and the all too human god on whom it would appear to be based. Does that, however, remove all need for the direct/indirect distinction in morals?

In view of the fact that, in Knauer's scheme of things, the moral rightness or wrongness of an act is determined by the presence or absence of a commensurate reason, his use of the direct/indirect terminology would seem to be an unnecessary complication. Grisez's objections to Knauer's theory, however, are not based on a love of simplicity. Knauer, he writes, ignores the fact that we are obliged not to turn directly against the good. Having made this omission, he finds the way open for his redefinition of "directly intended," which, says Grisez, bears no relation to previous uses of that expression.[45] What Grisez is saying here is not merely a repetition of the traditional direct/indirect distinction or an expression of his conviction that we must not do anything that the pope tells us not to do because the pope is God's mouthpiece. He has, instead, his own reasons for protesting, based on those "incommensurable" basic goods we examined in Chapter Four. In other words, although he fiercely defends deontological norms emanating from the Holy See, his reasons for keeping the direct/indirect distinction are not based on what some British and American philosophers might be inclined to call "the somewhat decorated naturalistic fallacy" of some recent popes. Indeed, Grisez avoids any accusation of naturalistic fallacy here. The foundation of his theory is formed by the basic *goods*.[46] His approach, therefore, though often referred to as "conservative," appears to be quite different from that of so-called official teaching.

It will be recalled that a basic principle of Grisez's theory is that, in moral choices, one must choose inclusivistically, in the sense that, when one is faced with a choice between two or more goods, one must acknowledge the values in the options not chosen, i.e., they are in no way downgraded. This basic principle of choosing inclusivistically takes shape by means of eight other principles which Grisez calls "modes of responsibility." The first such mode involves making consistent commitments. One should be committed to realizing basic purposes with which one can identify, in the sense that the acts through which they are realized help one to grow as a person. One's commitments should, moreover, be consistent with each other. The second mode of responsibility is the golden rule: "do unto others as you would have them do unto you." Number three is entitled "openness," that is, "willingness to help others, desire to see them develop and perfect themselves by realizing to the fullest the goods of which they are capable."[47] The fourth mode is detachment. The contrary of this would be such a strong attachment to one purpose that its loss or frustration is to the people concerned "a shattering experience which drains their lives of meaning."[48] If a person has a morally good attitude, he will not be so shattered by the loss because he will be open to all human goods. Number five is fidelity, remaining committed to one's ideals. The sixth mode he calls "pursuit of limited objectives." "Provided life is grounded upon and built around commitment to a consistent set of purposes, it is not only good sense but one's responsibility to put flesh, as it were, on the bones of commitments by pursuing specific, limited ends which really do further their realization."[49] Number seven is entitled "duties: responsibilities in community." This involves both contractual duties and the duties that arise from our social roles as members of communities.

We have described these seven modes of responsibility very briefly. The eighth mode, however, must be described in more detail, for it is when he comes to discuss this eighth mode of responsibility that Grisez poses the questions: "Is any action whatsoever allowable, at least in certain circumstances? Or are there actions which it is never morally right to perform?"[50] The eighth mode of responsibility, he says, demands an affirmative reply to the second question. And it is precisely here that "directness" acquires importance in Grisez's scheme of things.

> It may be put quite simply: It is never right to act directly against one of the fundamental human goods. "To act directly against a good" means to make a choice to destroy, damage or impede that good in one or more instances.[51]

Grisez admits that there can be cases of conflict. For instance, he says, a man's duties as husband and father may come into conflict with his responsibilities as employee. In a particular situation he may not be able to fulfill both duties. In such situations, writes Grisez, people must fulfill one set of duties and neglect the other. This they can do with a clear conscience because "these duties, while real, are not absolute responsibilities."[52] However, he continues, there are other responsibilities which do not arise from duties and are absolute. "They are founded on the implications of the ideal of openness to all the goods constitutive of the human person."[53] The basic human goods that go to make up personhood are the ends of human action and should not be treated as means to other ends. In its own way, each of these goods is the most important, and, therefore, may not be subordinated to any one of the others as a means to the achievement of that other good. Grisez explains what acting directly against one of the fundamental goods entails. When, he says, we are about to choose in a morally wrong way, we are about to perform an act which involves detriment to a human good and are inclined to accept that detriment because of the contribution it makes to the realization of another good. We thus decide that the good to be realized outweighs the good that will be damaged. However, says Grisez, those two goods are incommensurable. If we choose to act in this way, we cannot remain open to the good that will be damaged. We accept the violation of this good and, at least implicitly, adopt "a narrowed and restricted view of the purposes which go to make up human personhood: that is, of personhood itself." To act directly against one of the basic goods, he continues, is "to violate an actual or possible aspect of the personhood of a real person or persons." A human person is used as a means to an end.[54]

Where conflict is concerned, says Grisez, we should seek the solution by closely examining the structure of the action. If it directly realizes a human good and is an indivisible unity, the person who performs the act for the sake of that human good "need not be wrongly disposed toward the good which is simultaneously damaged."[55] Provided that he or she is not so disposed, the action might possibly be morally right. If, however, the good is obtained in an act other than the act in which the evil is caused, the two aspects are related as means and end, and the end does not justify the means. An example is the castration of boys to preserve their soprano voices. In such a case, says Grisez, the fundamental good of bodily integrity (part of the good of life) is subordinated to the aesthetic and religious goods. It is, he continues, immoral to subordinate one basic good to another or others. Castrating a boy who is suffering from a cancerous growth in the region of the testicles is, however, a different matter. There is no "means and end relationship" between the two aspects. Although the boy's bodily integrity is damaged, his life is protected in the very same act. One basic good is not being subordinated to another. If a cancerous womb is removed from a pregnant woman before the fetus is old enough to survive outside the womb, the death of the fetus is not the *means* to the mother's survival. It is an "unavoidable *side effect*, incidental to the lifesaving operation."[56]

Grisez, with all his talk of attitudes and the like, seems to concentrate more on the sphere of moral goodness than on the sphere of moral rightness. However, it is easy enough to see why he is opposed to proportionalism in general, and not just to Knauer's brand.

John M. Finnis makes a very similar analysis. In an article published in 1970, in which he acknowledges his debt to Grisez, he gives a list of basic values as follows:

> . . . living, in health and some security; the acquisition of arts and skills to be cultivated for their own sake; the relishing of beauty; the seeking of knowledge and understanding; the cultivation of friendships, immediate, communal and political; effective and intelligent freedom; a right relation in this passing life to the lasting principles of reality, "the gods"; the procreation of children and their education so that they can attain for themselves, and in their own mode, the foregoing values . . .[57]

If we are faced with the choice of either directly realizing or spurning one of these "irreducible values," we must, "in the Christian understanding,"[58] says Finnis, remain open to that value. That is the only reasonable way in which we can remain open to the ground of all values. If we act against that basic value in favor of another basic value, we act in an arbitrary fashion because "each of the basic values is equally basic, equally irreducibly and self-evidently attractive."[59] We must therefore always remain open to all the basic values.

> So: no suicide, no killing of the innocent: for human life is a fundamental value; no blasphemy: for a right relationship to God is a fundamental value; no injustice: for friendship in society is a fundamental value; no lying: for truth is a basic value and can be directly at stake in communication.[60]

Paul Ramsey writes in a somewhat similar vein, declaring that one should never directly attack the basic goods.[61] He also appeals to incommensurability as a reason for preserving the direct/indirect distinction. When we discuss the thought of W.D. Ross, he says, we often forget or lose sight of what Ross had to say about the discontinuity and incommensurability that exist among human goods. As examples, he cites the goods of happiness, the intellectual goods and moral good. It is not enough merely to say that moral good is higher up the scale than intellectual goods, and that the intellectual goods are, in their turn, higher up the scale than happiness. Where there is *only* a scale of goods to be taken into account, any conflict can in principle be resolved by having recourse to the scale: which is higher? which is lower? are they equal? Ross, however, was of the opinion, says Ramsey, that there was a great chasm or gulf between moral goodness and the intellectual goods, and another such chasm between the intellectual goods and happiness. One cannot justify any impairment of intellectual goods which is the price of an increase in happiness, says Ross. In the same way, no impairment of moral good or moral character can be justified by an augmentation of intellectual goods.

Had Ross recognized the fact that there are conflicts involving choices that reach across the chasm, and had he conceded the necessity of such choices, we may suppose, says Ramsey, that he might have said that one should not turn directly against moral good while pursuing intellectual goods, and that one should not turn directly against the "life of the mind" while pursuing moral goodness. And, of course, he might further have said that a person should not turn directly against the claims of reason while pursuing happiness, and should not turn directly against the good of happiness while pursuing intellectual values. All this can be supposed in spite of the fact that happiness may be considered a lower value than the intellectual goods and the intellectual goods lower than moral good. If Ross had admitted real indeterminacy in moral choice and the fact that some conflicts between *prima facie* duties could not be resolved into actual duties, he would have needed the distinction between willfully intending goods and consciously or willingly accepting the violations of other goods. The reason for this, says Ramsey, is not that one value is superior to another, that some values are absolute, or that some values are moral while others are nonmoral. The reason lies in the incommensurability of the values according to any single scale. "That stops any primary appeal to proportionate reason alone to resolve the ambiguities in moral choice."[62]

Another opponent of proportionalism, Paul Quay, takes a somewhat different stand. He insists on the importance of the cause/effect relationship, which, I imagine, could be renamed the "means/end relationship." If someone dies and I escape with my life, says Quay, the values in both cases would appear to be the same, all things being equal. That is the case whether there is a causal link between them or not. However, he continues, the moral importance of the other person's death being the cause of my escape is not negligible.[63] He recalls the permission "classically granted" to run down a child who is playing in a narrow road between cliff and chasm when a person is speeding along that road in a car, trying to escape from some people who are chasing him in another car and are intent on killing him. The case assumes, says Quay, that running down the child is necessary if the person fleeing is to escape with his life, but the child's death is not the cause of his staying alive. If, however, the road is wider and the child playing in the street is his pursuer's son, and the man fleeing runs him down, knowing that his enemy will most certainly call off the chase in such circumstances, then the child's death is the means or cause of his escape. If I put myself into this unenviable situation, "the question is not whether I cause the bad effect or not (I do by supposition) but whether the bad effect is causally related to the good intended."[64]

3. Some Counterarguments from the Proportionalist Camp

Although McCormick confesses to being "very sympathetic to Grisez's (philosophical) analysis of the origin of moral obligation,"[65] he most certainly does not come to the same conclusions on the question of the direct/indirect distinction. It is not clear to him, he writes, why a person must be said to turn against a basic good when he or she intends and effects evil as means.[66] Grisez says that the justification of an abortion to save the mother's life lies in the fact that the same indivisible act has both the good effect of saving life and the evil effect of destroying it. All aspects of the act are equally present to the agent at the moment of choosing.[67] McCormick, however, rather than seeing that as the justification, sees it as just one way of explaining how the evil is indirect "according to one understanding of what that term means."[68] It is the justification only if one assumes that a person who directly intends killing necessarily turns against a basic good, "that is, if directly intended killing is evil *in se.*"[69] In McCormick's mind the justification lies in the fact that the choice is between two alternatives, one of which is more destructive than the other. The choice is to abort or not to abort (and thereby leave both the mother and the fetus to die). He sees the justification in the fact that, all things considered, abortion is the lesser evil in this case. There is therefore a proportionate reason for the abortion, which can be called truly life-saving. "And is it not for this reason that abortion in these circumstances does not involve one in turning against a basic good?"[70] Grisez would not hesitate to choose in such a case, says McCormick, but, he asks, is not the "crucial and decisive consideration" the fact that it is better in such circumstances to save one life rather than to lose two (the only alternative). The procedure is legitimate, it would seem, for that very reason.

In brief, it is the presence or absence of a proportionate reason which determines whether my action—be it direct or indirect psychologically or causally—involves me in turning against a basic good in a way which is morally reprehensible.[71]

In another work published in the same year, McCormick says that the crucial question that has to be raised with both Grisez and Finnis is just what is to count as turning against a basic good and why. On this particular point he finds both of them unsatisfactory. Finnis says that there must be no killing of the innocent, but why does he include that word "innocent"? Even the lives of the criminally guilty are fundamental values. Finnis can insert the term "innocent" and in that way delimit the killings that involve choosing directly against a basic good because he has first weighed the life of the criminal, soldier, aggressor against other possible competitive and more urgent values and come to the conclusion that, when a human life is threatening a more urgent value, the taking of that life does not necessarily involve one in choosing directly against a basic good.[72]

When Finnis returned, in a later work, to his assertion that the innocence of the victim makes a difference when it comes to characterizing the killer's action as being open or not to the good of human life, McCormick declared: "Just how and why it makes a difference is difficult to unravel."[73] If, however, Finnis were to take a look at how the innocence or lack of innocence was applied in the past, for example, in the case of capital punishment, he would find "a consequentialist calculus at work in creating this exception."[74]

Addressing himself to Ramsey, McCormick writes that, because life is a basic good, he can accept the assertion that a person should never turn against life in the interest of another basic good. However, he does not see why the word "directly" should be added to the ban. The question at the very heart of the discussion, he says, is whether or not directly intended killing necessarily implies turning against the basic good of life. When Ramsey and Grisez assert that we should never turn *directly* against a basic good, instead of merely stating that we should never turn against a basic good (without the insertion of the word "directly"), they are adding nothing. "Indeed, they have suggested thereby the rather fuzzy possibility that one could only 'indirectly turn against the basic good'."[75] In the matter of a therapeutic abortion to save the mother's life in a case in which both mother and fetus would otherwise die, the only warrant for the intervention is the fact that taking one life is a lesser evil than losing two in these circumstances. "Ramsey's subsequent appeal to indirectness is precisely that, subsequent—tacked on, in the interests of getting the killing within the reach of a distinction whose moral relevance he has accepted, but never explained."[76]

With regard to Ramsey's problem of incommensurability, McCormick states that he can agree with Ross that we are faced with great difficulties when we try to commeasure good things of different types, but those difficulties, he holds, are not insuperable. We do, in fact, commensurate. For example, we go to war to protect freedom. In other words, we are willing to sacrifice life for the good of freedom. If that does not involve commensurating, says McCormick, "then I do not know what commensurating means."[77] The fact is, he continues, we do measure or weigh the apparently incommensurable.[78]

As for Quay's arguments, some interesting points are made by Franz Scholz in an article in which he does not in fact address himself specifically to Quay.[79] Scholz discusses the killing of innocent persons in the bombardment of an enemy fortress. The commanding officer may well wish that no innocents (noncombatants, civilians) be harmed, but it is a vain wish, and he knows very well that the bombs or shells will strike soldiers, civilians, animals and property without distinction. His vain wish implies only that the deaths of the civilians are not *propter se* but *propter aliud*. In practice, however, those deaths are the *sine qua non* for the achievement of the principal goal. What happens always and necessarily as the result of an action cannot be excluded from the intention. We can only speak about true side effects when there is another cause at work. Killing the civilians is therefore, in this case, direct.[80] Scholz also examines another example taken from the manuals. It is an ancient version of the example discussed by Quay. An unarmed knight meets his well-armed deadly enemy. He tries to escape by galloping away on his horse. At one point where the road is very narrow his way is blocked by crippled and blind people, people who cannot move quickly out of his way. Any deaths caused by the escaping knight in this situation were traditionally described as accidental. This was made possible, says Scholz, by limiting the object of the act to "riding a horse" or "escaping on a horse along a road." But how can we exclude the essential circumstances of the presence of the blind and crippled people from the object of the act, he asks. Killing those people is the means to the end of saving the life of the unarmed knight. And means, like ends, can only be intended directly. We could speak of a real side effect in such a case if the victims threw themselves under the horse's hooves at the last moment.[81] A true side effect is had, continues Scholz, in the case of scandal[82] where my act does not cause my neighbor's wrongdoing. Another cause comes into play for that: my neighbor's own act.[83]

4. Disagreement within the Proportionalist Camp

All proportionalists, it would seem, would find themselves disagreeing with Grisez, Finnis, Ramsey and Quay on the subject of the direct/indirect distinction in morals. However, they have not always been in complete agreement on the subject among themselves, as will become apparent in the following pages.

In an article first published in German in 1972,[84] Schüller sees the direct/indirect distinction as important in cases involving leading another person into sin. However, when it comes to acts like self-killing and the use of contraceptives, acts which traditional moral theology branded as intrinsically evil, he regards the distinction as useless. Why so? We can understand the norm that we should not lead another into sin, he writes, only if we know exactly what is meant by the word "lead." If we accept that leading another into sin means making a free decision which you foresee will have the sin of another as a consequence, the prohibition could be worded thus: "You shall not make a decision from which you know that it will have as a consequence the moral transgression of another."[85] However, says Schüller, such a norm would establish as illicit acts which we would be inclined to regard as licit or even morally obligatory. A civil legislator may foresee, for example, that the passing of any new penal law will *lead* an indefinite number of people to the sin of blackmailing other people who break those laws. According to the wording of the above norm, the legislator would therefore not be permitted to pass any penal laws. This, says Schüller, is obviously absurd. In order to avoid such absurdity, we must resort to the permitting or tolerating will. In other words, the direct/indirect distinction would appear to be necessary here. Leading another into sin, in the way in which this is understood in moral theology, is morally evil by its very nature. It has the sin of another person as its foreseen and intended consequence. Such an act is a direct (formal) leading into sin. If, on the other hand, one person's act results in another person's sin, but that sin is merely allowed, the act can, under certain conditions, be permitted or even be obligatory. It is an indirect leading into sin.[86]

The permissive will and the indirect act are therefore required as "ethically meaningful categories" for moral evil, continues Schüller. It is the absoluteness of the disvalue concerned (sin) which makes the distinction necessary. However, when it comes to nonmoral evils, such as death, error, sickness and pain, the absoluteness disappears. We may cause a relative disvalue (and there are times when we *should* cause one) if it is necessary for the realization of a preferable value. In such a case, one might like to say that the causing of the disvalue is like an indirect act, merely allowed as a side effect. In doing so, however, one would have to resort to "linguistic convulsions" that most people would regard as unusual, if not downright nonsensical. An example is that of the health police forcing quarantine on someone who has caught typhus. We should have to say that the health police intend only to prevent an outbreak of typhus. They merely permit or "regretfully tolerate" the isolation that they have forced upon the sick person. If we were to use ordinary language in discussing such a case, we would say that the causing of the evil serves a good end and would be a necessary means to that end. Schüller wonders why we should stray from such ordinary speech.

> It is not easy to see why one should abandon this way of speaking. On the contrary, this way of speaking expresses clearly the differing attitude one should have toward moral evil and non-moral evil. For the sake of a correspondingly important good, one may merely permit a *moral* evil or cause it indirectly. But he may intentionally desire and directly cause the non-moral evil.[87]

This would even apply in the case of material cooperation in the sin of another. One should not, of course, indulge in formal cooperation. That would consist in approving of the sin and "sharing in its performance." However, in the case of material cooperation, one is concerned only with nonmoral evil. A cashier in a bank, for example, is faced with the alternative of handing over the cash or being shot. The robber's moral guilt will not be affected by the decision of the cashier. It will not be greater or less as a result of his or her decision. However, by handing over the cash to the robber, the cashier keeps nonmoral evil to a minimum. Schüller sees no need to resort to categories such as "nonintended" or "indirect" consequences of the cashier's act. He or she should simply hand over the cash to the robber because that is a lesser nonmoral evil than the loss of human life.

Schüller and the deontologists find themselves in disagreement in only a very small area. Where omissions and indirect acts are concerned, writes Schüller, even so-called deontologists decide for or against the omission or indirect act on teleological grounds: is there a proportionate reason? It is only in such spheres as direct killing of the innocent, killing oneself, and the performance of certain activities in the sexual sphere—as, for example, the use of contraceptives—that differences arise. That is because these last mentioned acts are described by deontologists as intrinsically evil on the grounds that they have the characteristic either of arrogation of a right reserved to God or of being contrary to nature. Teleologists, however, would deny this. If, therefore, you are a teleologist, says Schüller, the distinction between a direct act and an indirect act can only be ethically meaningful for you "if, and only if, the consequence of the act is in itself morally evil."[88]

Having favorably reviewed this article of Schüller's in his "Notes on Moral Theology," McCormick took a look at the origins of the direct/indirect terminology. It could be argued, he said, that those origins are to be found in the value conflicts which are inevitable in human choosing. If an important value or good could be effected only by causing harm, then the performance of such an act was judged morally proper if the chosen good was of greater, or at least equal, importance to the unavoidable harm. "In other words, there was a proportionate reason for choosing the disvalue. The disvalue was not to be imputed to me precisely because it was unavoidable."[89] What is not to be imputed to a person is not part of that person's purposes and aims in the same way as that which is imputed is part of them. This nonimputable choice therefore began to be called *indirecte voluntarium*. "Indirect" was first of all a way of saying that proportion existed between the value pursued and the value left undone or the disvalue caused. "It was not primarily a psychological analysis."[90] Later, however, continues McCormick, the terms "direct" and "indirect" took on a psychological interpretation and "became terms which decided what actions are licit or illicit rather than terms used to summarise such a conclusion drawn on other grounds (presence or absence of proportionate reason)."[91]

Clearly, however, McCormick had second thoughts on the subject. Because both direct and indirect causing of nonmoral evil are to be judged teleologically, it does not follow, he writes in a later work, that the same teleological judgment applies to both of them. It does not seem to follow that a proportionate reason for causing harm in an indirect way will be a proportionate reason for causing it in a direct way. "In other words, there may be a proportionate reason for doing something in one way which is not proportionate to doing it another way."[92] As an example, he cites the killing of noncombatants in wartime. Traditional theology says that it may at times be permissible to attack the enemy even though noncombatants will be killed in the process. The same traditional moral theology, however, forbids making noncombatants the target of one's attack, the aim being to destroy morale, to weaken the enemy's will to fight. McCormick believes that this latter conclusion is based on teleological grounds: direct attacks on noncombatants "will in the long run release more violence and be more destructive to human life than the lives we might save by directly attacking noncombatants."[93]

This assessment, however, teleological though it is, is different from the teleological assessment made when the deaths of noncombatants are incidental. The number of deaths here and now could be the same in both cases, but *how* those deaths occur "has a good deal to say about the present meaning of the action, the effect on the agent and others, and hence about the protection and security of life in the long run."[94] In the case of the rioting mob and the judge,[95] it would seem, says McCormick, that Schüller would be forced to conclude that the innocent man should be executed, "if his analysis stops where it does."[96] We are appalled at this because we feel that taking an innocent man's life in such circumstances "would represent a capitulation to and encouragement of a type of injustice which in the long run would render many more lives vulnerable."[97] If, however, the man's death were incidental, our judgment might be different.

> In summary, proportion must be measured also in terms of long term effects. And in terms of such effects, whether one directly intends (or not) certain non-moral evils he now does may make quite a difference.[98]

Perhaps the key to McCormick's misgivings is to be found in his assertion that "an intending will represents a closer relation of the agent to the disvalue and therefore indicates a greater willingness that the disvalue occur."[99]

In his reply, Schüller declares that he is prepared to grant a *"prima facie* plausibility" to McCormick's view. That view is, he says, that in some cases, and only in some, all other relevant factors being equal, direct killing leads to long-term consequences which differ significantly from the consequences resulting from indirect killing, and this difference is in some way due to the directness and indirectness of the killings. However, says Schüller, in view of the fact that McCormick admits that the results of the two kinds of killings do not always, but only sometimes, differ, "he is forced to claim that it is not indirectness of killing alone, but indirectness contingently combined with one or other factor that accounts for a morally significant difference in consequences."[100]

With regard to killing noncombatants in time of war, Schüller asks if it is reasonable to use the term "indirect" in the example used by McCormick when the latter refers to attacking the enemy's war machine, "even though some noncombatants (innocents) will be tragically and regretfully killed in the process."[101] If, says Schüller, a regiment can gain a certain tactical position only by killing some noncombatants, such killing is, according to traditional standards, direct. If we apply the traditional way of distinguishing direct killing from indirect killing, we find that soldiers could often transform the former into the latter by using more destructive weapons. If they use heavy artillery against the enemy, they can say that any killing of civilians is indirect. If, however, they use small arms fire, they may have to kill some noncombatants first (i.e., before the combatants) in order to be able to repel the enemy's attack. In other words, the civilians are killed directly merely because the soldiers do not have at hand the heavy artillery necessary to kill them at the same time as the soldiers, and therefore indirectly.

Killing civilians as a means of destroying your enemy's morale and weakening his will to fight strikes Schüller as being morally wrong, but not because it is direct. Such killing he sees as bearing a family resemblance to taking hostages and political kidnapping. There would appear to be a "*prima facie* wrongfulness," he says, in repelling unjust aggression by inflicting harm on your aggressor's relatives and friends when they do not form a part of the aggression. In short,

> No doubt, in warfare direct and indirect killing of civilians have relatively different results; however, there are some other things that are *unequal*. Direct killing is either scarcely ever necessary or it is a means of extortion. Moreover, the principle of *moderamen inculpatae tutelae* seems best suited to explain why, given these inequalities, direct and indirect killing are to be judged differently.[102]

Schüller then turns his attention to McCormick's claim that "an intending will represents a closer relation of the agent to the disvalue and therefore indicates a greater willingness that the disvalue occur." Where another person's wrongdoing is concerned, he says, permitting and intending it are related to one another in the manner of contrary opposites.[103] There is only one alternative to approval of moral wrongness, and that is disapproval. It follows, therefore, that permitting another person's wrong-doing means disapproving of it but not preventing it. When someone decides for an immoral way of life, decides to be bad (sin in the strict sense of the word), there is nothing we can do to prevent it. However, we are frequently in a position to hinder the wrongdoing (actions causing more nonmoral harm than is inevitable) of other people. However, "some-one who disapproves of unnecessary harm being produced cannot, without inconsistency, be willing to hinder another's causing unnecessary harm if by hindering it he could not help making the situation still worse."[104] When we turn from the intending or permitting of wrong behavior to the intending or permitting of nonmoral evil, we find that the demarcation line is not to be found neatly separating intending from permitting. Instead, it runs between intending as end on the one hand, and intending or permitting as means on the other. Now Schüller is inclined to believe that " 'intend as a means' and 'permit,' when referring to a nonmoral evil, denote exactly the same mental attitude."[105] This belief is supported, he claims, by McCormick himself, who raises what Schüller regards as an "insuperable difficulty" against his own account: "The person who is prepared to realize the good even by intending the evil is more willing that the good exist."[106]

In his reply, McCormick presented a somewhat revised argument. He accepted Schüller's thesis that permitting nonmoral evil as a means and intending it can belong to the same moral category because the agent may disapprove of the evil but consider it unavoidable in both cases, whereas intending as an end implies approval. He went on to say that we can expect unnecessary harm to have deleterious effects. The wrong-fulness of the acts under discussion, however, is not determined by those effects. It is, he said, the lack of proportion that determines their wrong-fulness. The value being pursued is being pursued in a way that will undermine it. McCormick tentatively sought the explanation of the dis-proportion in an association of basic goods. The way in which one good is protected or pursued brings other goods into play and could thus be responsible for disproportion. He therefore chose to abandon his long-term effect explanation of teleology, but saw no reason for abandoning the teleology itself.[107]

Schüller had denied McCormick's allegation that in the case of the rioting mob and the judge he would be forced to conclude that the innocent man should be executed. As we saw in the last chapter, Schüller's argument (insufficient in the opinion of the present author)[108] was that the whole institution of criminal law was at stake. McCormick returned to that case.

Protecting human life by framing an innocent man, he says, would, in the long run, undermine that very value which is being protected, by causing serious harm to another good (human liberty) which is associated to the good of life. He argues that, if we kill one innocent person to prevent other people from killing five innocent persons, we deny the freedom of those other people. That, he says, is the moral meaning of extortion. If I suppose that another person's cessation of wrongdoing is dependent upon my doing harm, I deny and undermine human freedom. "And because such freedom is an associated good upon which the very good of life itself depends, undermining it in the manner of my defence of life is undermining life itself—is disproportionate."[109] There is no weighing of life against freedom here he says. "One merely associates the associable and reads proportion within such an interrelationship."[110] In the classic abortion case where the doctor is faced with the choice of aborting the fetus and thus saving the mother or not aborting and thus allowing both mother and fetus to die, there is an essential connection between aborting and saving the mother's life. In the case of the rioting mob, there is no such essential connection. In warfare there is no necessary connection between killing noncombatants as a morale-breaking exercise and the enemy's ceasing his unjust aggression.[111]

Lisa Cahill is not totally satisfied with this. McCormick, she declares, formulated his arguments about the association of basic goods and the requirement of necessity in order to preclude the killing of innocents for utilitarian reasons. However, she continues, it is questionable that they are the logical results of his theory.[112] John Langan goes further in his criticism. Such a formulation, he says, forbids too much. McCormick says that there is no necessary connection between killing noncombatants and the enemy's ceasing his unjust aggression, but neither is there any *necessary* connection between killing enemy soldiers and the enemy's cessation of his aggression. Such a requirement would therefore rule out the killing of combatants as well as noncombatants. The same requirement that there be a necessary connection also permits too much, for, says Langan, there is reason to think that there *is* a necessary connection between destroying a whole nation and the enemy's cessation of his aggression. McCormick might say that all attacks aiming at the destruction of whole societies are morally wrong because the evil done outweighs the good achieved. That is true, says Langan, but he would still argue that, "given a nondeterministic understanding of human freedom," there is no necessary connection between a person's action and the free reactions of other people. Rather than needing a necessary connection requirement, he sees the theory of proportionate reason in need of a principle holding that harm done to another person to prevent his doing evil should not be more than is needed "to dissuade him or, if that fails, to disable him."[113]

Without a doubt one of the most prolific writers in the whole debate on proportionalism, McCormick came back yet again. In the case of self-defense or warfare, he wrote, the necessary connection is not between killing the aggressor(s) and the cessation of aggression. It is between self-defense and killing aggressors. Once aggression has begun, the use of force is the only way to achieve defense. Killing my aggressor's wife may in fact achieve cessation of aggression, but in that case there is no necessary connection between defense and the harm done. As for Langan's call for a principle of moderation, McCormick points out that it is first necessary to show that it is morally acceptable to harm *at all*. He goes on to add, however, that he is far from sure that the necessary connection requirement is valid.[114]

5. Comments and Conclusions

Everyone involved in the debate, it would seem, is wary of a too physical interpretation of the direct/indirect distinction which could all too easily lead to a description of certain morally wrong acts as morally right. An example would be the unnecessary removal of the uterus in the case of a therapeutic abortion so as not to touch the fetus directly.

Another interpretation of the distinction is that it refers to intending. Now, we have seen that, in traditional Catholic moral theology, only the reason for the act is intended, and everything else is unintended. In the case of a therapeutic abortion to save the mother, only the saving of the mother would be intended. The killing of the fetus would be unintended. However, that is not really at all helpful. Here, as in every other case, the reason for acting is good. We still need to ask: is it right or wrong to kill the fetus? The answer must be: it is right if there is a proportionate reason. The direct/indirect distinction thus far is useless.

Knauer adds something to the above analysis. He says that, if there is no proportionate reason for the act, the evil in the act becomes part of the reason and is therefore directly intended. However, in practice, he is saying nothing more than: if there is no proportionate reason, the act is a morally wrong one. Any talk of directly or indirectly intending would seem to be an unnecessary addition.

What happens, then, when we turn to that school of thought led by

Grisez which holds that we must not turn directly against a basic good? Turning against a basic good is an attitude in Grisez's scheme of things. It is equivalent to turning against goodness, which is, of course, sin. Grisez, therefore, does not tell us how to work out what is right and what is wrong. In their discussion he and McCormick are talking about different things.[115] A conversation of that kind could continue going around in circles indefinitely.

As for McCormick's necessary connection requirement, there would appear to be no grounds for seeing that as anything more than an unnecessary complication. His reply to Langan really involves little more than playing with words when it is submitted to scrutiny. The necessary connection in warfare, he says, is not between killing the aggressors and the cessation of aggression, but between self-defense and killing aggressors. Well, then, can we not reasonably suppose that, in a war between A and B, there is a necessary connection between A's self-defense and the total annihilation of B by the use of nuclear weapons? In the end we are still left with the lack of a proportionate reason as the deciding factor.

It is, however, still possible that McCormick is right in thinking that Schüller's reduction of the range of usefulness of the direct/indirect distinction is just a little too drastic. Suppose we take the term "direct" to signify "the performance of an external act," and "indirect" to signify "anything which flows from that act (or the results of setting a series of events into motion)."[116] I remember once hearing Josef Fuchs refer in conversation to the fact of our being less responsible for some indirect effects than we are for more direct ones. If "direct" and "indirect" are understood in the above senses, then, of course, we most certainly cannot be held as responsible for improbable, unforeseen, or unforeseeable effects as we are for more direct ones. The use of the word "more" may even be important here because there does seem to be a case for talking about degrees of directness or indirectness. For example, effects which occur as the result of the free reaction of another person to a certain act could be said to be more indirect than effects which we would normally expect to flow from such an act (i.e., without the reaction or intervention of another person). However, it should be pointed out that, when it comes to the making of moral judgments and decisions (before the event), although we can and should take improbable effects into account, we do not take unforeseen and unforeseeable effects into account, precisely because they are unforeseen. This is another indication of our fallibility, even when we act in good faith.

As for leading another into sin, Schüller says that if an act results in another's sin, but that is merely allowed, the act may be licit under certain circumstances. "It is called," he says, "an indirect leading another into sin." The direct/indirect distinction here coincides with the moral goodness/rightness distinction, or rather the moral badness/wrongness distinction. Leading another person into sin in the sense of deliberately guiding that person towards sin (direct leading) is necessarily sinful, and therefore outside the scope of proportionalism. A question still remains, however, about indirect leading into sin. Is there a possible objection here to the proportionalists' claim that they balance only *premoral* goods and evils against each other? In other words, do I weigh the premoral goods I aim at against the possibility of a moral evil being committed by someone else? Do I weigh premoral goods and evils against moral goods and evils? Indeed, no. I cannot prevent another person's sin. What I can sometimes prevent is the premoral evil in another person's wrongdoing, and such a possibility should enter into my "calculations." However, it should be pointed out that, often, such a consideration cannot carry a great deal of weight. We could, for instance, end up in the absurd situation of never making anything of beauty or worth because of the possibility that somebody might steal it. This is close to what we said above regarding our not being as responsible for unforeseeable indirect effects as we are for more direct ones.

Notes

1. P. Knauer, "The Hermeneutic Function. . . ," 1.
2. Ibid.
3. Ugorji writes about the principle of double effect: "Its use is rather restricted to an act with a double moral character; an act may be said to be right insofar as it produces a value and always wrong insofar as it produces an intrinsic (moral) evil" (L.I. Ugorji, *The Principle of Double Effect. A Critical Appraisal of Its Traditional Understanding and Its Modern Interpretation* (Frankfurt, 1985), 53). Such confusing use of the terms "right," "wrong" and "moral evil" does not help to clarify the meaning of the principle. An act cannot be both right and wrong. One assumes that the meaning given to "moral evil" here is "evil produced in a morally wrong act." We have already seen McCormick referring to premoral evil becoming moral evil in that way. The present author prefers to restrict the meaning of the term "moral evil" to "sin," and "sin," of course, should be understood here in the formal sense.
4. I have chosen Selling's formulation here (J.A. Selling, "The Problem of Reinterpreting the Principle of Double Effect," *Louvain Studies* 8 (1980): 48). He adds in a

footnote that the actual formulation often differs from one author to another, even in the standardized handbooks (ibid., footnote 4). For examples of other formulations, see Ugorji, op. cit., 29–30.

5. That would appear to be McCormick's interpretation in *Ambiguity in Moral Choice*.

6. J.A. Selling, art. cit., 59.

7. Ibid., 59–60. The final sentence is printed thus.

8. Ibid., 52.

9. We have already had occasion to refer to the strangeness of such a "condition." See note 6.

10. L.I. Ugorji, op. cit., 30–31.

11. Ibid., 28.

12. Ibid., 139.

13. J.A. Selling, art. cit., 51.

14. See ibid., 52. Sometimes, however, writers confuse "intention" with "voluntariety." Albert Di Ianni, for example, writes that the "central nerve" of the principle of double effect "is the notion that evil should never be the object of direct intention whether as an end (*per se et propter se*) or as a means to a good end (*per se sed non propter se*). Three of the four well-known conditions for legitimate application of the principle are aimed at insuring indirect voluntariety (a permitting rather than an intending will) relative to an act which one foresees will have both a good and an evil effect" (A. Di Ianni, "The Direct/Indirect Distinction in Morals," in *Readings . . . No. 1*, 215).

15. G. Kelly, "Notes on Moral Theology," *Theological Studies* 14 (1953): 40–41.

16. J. McCarthy, *Problems in Theology II: The Commandments* (Dublin, 1960), 122.

17. J.A. Selling, art. cit., 53.

18. J. Murtagh, *Intrinsic Evil* (Rome, 1973), 30. See *AAS* 22 (1930): 559. Murtagh also points out, however, that in 1853, when dealing with the question of whether or not a wife may passively offer herself in intercourse when her husband is using a condom, the Holy Office of the Inquisition replied that to do so would be to take part in "what is intrinsically unlawful" (J. Murtagh, op. cit., 29–30).

19. *AAS*, Vol. 43 (1951): 843.

20. *AAS*, Vol. 48 (1956): 472.

21. J. Murtagh, op. cit., 31.

22. Ibid. (emphasis mine). See Paul VI, *Humanae Vitae*, *AAS* 60 (1968): 491.

23. J. Murtagh, op. cit., 59.

24. Ibid., 59–60.

25. Ibid., 60–61.

26. Ibid., 65.

27. Ibid., 70.

28. J. Fuchs, "An Ongoing Discussion in Christian Ethics: 'Intrinsically Evil Acts'?," in *Christian Ethics in a Secular Arena*, 74.

29. Nothing like the same amount of attention seems to be devoted to nonverbal communication, in spite of the importance attributed to it in modern psychology.

30. B. Schüller, "Various Types of Grounding for Ethical Norms," 187.

31. Ibid.

32. Ibid., 187–88. Fuchs makes the same point, distinguishing God's will as Creator from his moral will: "The *moral* will of God, and therefore a natural law obligation, is not indicated in the nature and the natural finality of a particular act; rather moral rightness

has to be discovered by a moral judgment, and this potential has been given by God to human beings. Moral rightness is not discovered through the natural finality of human sexuality or human speech; rather it resides in the capacity of human beings to make moral judgments" (J. Fuchs, "An Ongoing Discussion. . . ," 78).

33. B. Schüller, "Various Types. . . ," 188.

34. J. Fuchs, "Das Gottesbild und die Moral innerweltlichen Handelns," *Stimmen der Zeit* 202 (1984): 363–82. Not yet published in English translation.

35. Ibid., 379–81.

36. Ibid., 382.

37. G. Grisez, *The Way of the Lord Jesus. Vol. 1, Christian Moral Principles* (Chicago, 1983), 570.

38. Ibid., 571.

39. Ibid., 566.

40. Ibid., 566–67.

41. Ibid., 899.

42. Ibid., 850.

43. Ibid., 853. Although it is often difficult to pinpoint exactly what he is getting at, it would appear that, at least sometimes, the Protestant theologian Paul Ramsey falls into the trap of reducing morality to obedience to God's rules. Naturally, he does not feel bound by the statements of the Catholic magisterium, but he does feel bound by the deontological precepts he sees arising from sinful man's relationship with the righteous God. Agape springs from this righteous God, he says, and man must conform to the rules that this agape defines. If anybody got the impression from his early work *Basic Christian Ethics* that Ramsey could be interpreted as a teleologist, that impression was dashed in a later work. "If agapism is *not* a third and a distinctive type of normative theory which is neither teleology (goal-seeking) nor deontology (an ethics of duty) then it seems to me more true to say that it is a type of deontology. Agape defines for the Christian what is right, righteous, obligatory to be done among men; it is not a Christian's definition of the good that better be done and much less is it a definition of the right way to be good . . . The Christian understanding of righteousness is therefore radically non-teleological. It means ready obedience to the *present* reign of God, the alignment of the human will with the Divine will that men should live together in covenant love no matter what the morrow brings, or if it brings nothing. When Christ comes he will ask whether there is any faith and love in the earth, not whether there is any practice of the principle of benevolence, i.e., doing good" (P. Ramsey, *Deeds and Rules in Christian Ethics* (Edinburgh, 1965), 96–97).

44. That does not, of course, mean that the term "intrinsic evil" should disappear from moral theology.

45. G. Grisez, *Abortion: The Myths, the Realities and the Arguments* (New York, 1970), 331.

46. As Janice Schultz puts it, Grisez holds that " 'oughts' arise from 'goods'." J.L. Schultz, "Is–Ought: Prescribing and a Present Controversy," *The Thomist* 49 (1985): 4.

47. G. Grisez and R. Shaw, *Beyond the New Morality*, 115.

48. Ibid., 116.

49. Ibid., 118.

50. Ibid., 135.

51. Ibid., 135–36.

52. Ibid., 136. If a person may neglect his or her duties with a clear conscience,

they are most certainly *not* duties. W.D. Ross's expression *"prima facie* duty" overcomes this difficulty.

53. Ibid.

54. Ibid., 138.

55. Ibid., 147–48.

56. Ibid., 153 (emphasis his).

57. J.M. Finnis, "Natural Law and Unnatural Acts," *The Heythrop Journal* 11 (1970): 367. Finnis leaves the list thus, apparently incomplete. In a later work he presents a list of seven basic goods which is very similar to Grisez's list but does not include "integrity" (also called "wholeness," "inner harmony" and, somewhat colloquially, "getting it all together"). See J.M. Finnis, *Natural Law and Natural Rights* (Oxford, 1980), 90. Some scholars might well wonder just how exhaustive these lists are.

58. Ibid., 375. Are we to assume from this that a non-Christian understanding would lead to a different conclusion? On page 376 of the *Heythrop Journal* article, Finnis writes: "This paper is an effort of *fides quaerens intellectum.*" Are we to conclude, however, that, when Finnis is not theologizing, any purely philosophical work he produces on this particular subject is for Christian eyes only?

59. Ibid.

60. Ibid., 376. What Finnis says on the subject is, of course, very close indeed to Grisez's approach. Another "disciple" of Grisez would appear to be William E. May. See, for example, his *Human Existence, Medicine and Ethics* (Chicago, 1977), 10–12.

61. P. Ramsey, "Incommensurability and Indeterminacy in Moral Choice," in *Doing Evil to Achieve Good*, 91–92.

62. Ibid., 90–91.

63. P.M. Quay, "Morality by Calculation of Values," in *Readings . . . No. 1*, 276.

64. Ibid., 285.

65. R.A. McCormick, "A Commentary on the Commentaries," 213.

66. R.A. McCormick, *Ambiguity in Moral Choice*, 45.

67. G. Grisez, *Abortion: The Myths. . . ,* 340.

68. R.A. McCormick, *Ambiguity. . . ,* 49.

69. Ibid.

70. Ibid., 50.

71. Ibid., 53.

72. R.A. McCormick, *Notes . . . 1965 through 1980*, 453.

73. Ibid., 506. The work referred to is J. Finnis, "The Rights and Wrongs of Abortion," *Philosophy and Public Affairs* 2 (1973): 117–45.

74. Ibid. The following year found McCormick grappling with Connery's assertion that Fuchs, Schüller and others were tending toward consequentialism. To avoid misunderstandings, it would seem, he became much more careful about the use of expressions like "consequentialist calculus" in his subsequent writings. This is a good example of how the "opposition party" helped the proportionalists to clear their own thinking on certain issues.

75. R.A. McCormick, "A Commentary on the Commentaries," 214.

76. Ibid. McCormick goes on to point out that, unlike Grisez and Finnis, Ramsey does not give us a list of basic goods. "At one place he says one ought not turn against 'any human good' . . . Ramsey even refers to turning 'directly against the value of Russian nationhood,' whatever that might mean" (ibid.).

77. Ibid., 227.

78. Ibid., 228.

79. F. Scholz, "Possibilità e impossibilità dell agire indiretto," in *Fede cristiana e agire morale,* ed. K. Demmer and B. Schüller (Assisi, 1980). This is the Italian version of "Objekt und Umstande, Wesenswirkungen und Nebeneffekte," in *Christlich Glauben und Handeln,* which the present author does not have to hand. To the best of my knowledge, this article has never been published in English translation.

80. Ibid., 306–07.

81. Ibid., 303–06.

82. As opposed to seduction.

83. Ibid., 307–08.

84. B. Schüller, "Direkte Tötung—Indirekte Tötung," *Theologie und Philosophie* 47 (1972): 341–57. It was later published in English as "Direct Killing/Indirect Killing," in *Readings . . . No. 1,* 138–57.

85. B. Schüller, "Direct Killing/Indirect Killing," 141.

86. Ibid., 142.

87. Ibid., 144 (emphasis mine).

88. Ibid., 155.

89. R.A. McCormick, *Notes . . . 1965 through 1980,* 352.

90. Ibid.

91. Ibid., 353.

92. R.A. McCormick, *Ambiguity in Moral Choice,* 58–59.

93. Ibid., 59–60.

94. Ibid., 60.

95. See the section on justice in Chapter Four.

96. R.A. McCormick, *Ambiguity in Moral Choice,* 63.

97. Ibid., 63–64.

98. Ibid., 64.

99. Ibid., 65.

100. B. Schüller, "The Double Effect in Catholic Thought: A Reevaluation," 179.

101. R.A. McCormick, *Ambiguity in Moral Choice,* 59.

102. B. Schüller, "The Double Effect. . . ," 182.

103. Ibid., 190.

104. Ibid., 188.

105. Ibid., 191.

106. R.A. McCormick, *Ambiguity in Moral Choice,* 88.

107. R.A. McCormick, "A Commentary on the Commentaries," 264–65.

108. See the section on justice in Chapter Four.

109. R.A. McCormick, *Notes . . . 1965 through 1980,* 720. Here he is summarizing his own article: "Il principio del duplice effetto," *Concilium* 12/10 (1976): 1723–1743. It was also published in German, French, Spanish and Dutch, but not in English.

110. Ibid.

111. Ibid., 722.

112. L.S. Cahill, "Teleology, Utilitarianism and Christian Ethics," *Theological Studies* 42 (1981): 624.

113. J. Langan, "Direct and Indirect—Some Recent Exchanges between Paul Ramsey and Richard McCormick," *Religious Studies Review* 5 (1979): 100.

114. R.A. McCormick, *Notes . . . 1965 through 1980,* 812.

115. All too often, discussions between scholars are reminiscent of the Frenchman and the Italian, neither of whom understood the other's language. "Vous ne voulez pas comprendre," roared the exasperated Frenchman. "Ha ragione," replied the wary Italian. "Non voglio comprare niente."

116. See footnote 17.

CHAPTER SIX

Conclusions to Be Drawn and Comments to Be Made

Perhaps one of the most remarkable conclusions to be drawn from the foregoing analysis is the fact that, although proportionalism has been seen by many as something of a revolution, it is really not as new as it might at first appear to be. Indeed, the need for a proportionate reason is one of the most deeply rooted elements in the tradition of Catholic moral theology. Protestations about the incommensurability of values could seem to make nonsense of that tradition. We have seen, however, that such protestations themselves make sense only if we reduce ethics to the level of mathematics and human beings to the level of computers. It is not merely tradition but common sense that dictates the need for a proportionate reason. As Cardinal Joseph Ratzinger (himself no supporter of proportionalism) puts it:

> The attempt to assess the proportion of the good or bad likely to proceed from a proposed action is really a common-sense judgment we all make rather routinely. Even the principle of totality and the whole tradition of examining the circumstances of an act employs a notion of proportionality and, I think, with some effect.[1]

In the same way we can say that, as teleologists, the proportionalists are not at all unusual in the Catholic Church. It would be wrong to see them demanding a shift from a deontological way of thinking to a more teleological one. Catholic moral theology has always been predominantly teleological. However, it must be admitted that there are examples of widely taught deontological norms of behavior in the formulation of which the teleological aspects have either been ignored or not considered important enough to be taken into consideration. This is seen, for example, in the ban on telling untruths even to save the life of one's neighbor. What the proportionalists have done is point out the inconsistency and invalidity of such thinking.

In the debate on proportionalism an understandable fear of utilitarianism has clouded some of the issues involved in the deontology/teleology distinction. The greater emphasis on teleological elements led some critics of proportionalism to see it as a form of utilitarianism or consequentialism. Because utilitarianism cannot be used to deal with cases of justice and promise keeping, it was assumed that proportionalism would run into the same difficulties. We have seen, however, that such elements as the premoral evil of breaking a promise or the injustice in a situation must be taken into account when using proportionalism to establish the rightness or wrongness of a proposed action, as must all other premoral goods and premoral evils.

In spite of the emphasis put on the rightness/goodness distinction in the present work, it must be admitted that here too the proportionalists are not introducing anything totally new to Catholic moral theology. The distinction between formal sin and material sin was essentially the same thing. What is involved is merely a change in terminology, but one which leads to far greater clarity and far less confusion. Unfortunately, however, as we have seen, the importance of the distinction has not always been appreciated. Thus we find people on both sides of the debate apparently discussing the use of proportionalism to judge the heart of the person acting. It should be clear by now that proportionalism can be used to judge nothing of the kind. The moral goodness of the person is, of course, the chief concern of moral theology. Proportionalism, however, is concerned only with the secondary aspect, which is, of course, intimately linked to the primary one, but not to be confused with it. That secondary aspect is the rightness or wrongness of actions. What the church teaches regarding salvation and moral goodness comes from Revelation, and that she teaches infallibly. In the area of moral rightness and wrongness, however, mistakes can all too easily be made. Proportionalism is an attempt to cut down the number of those mistakes, an attempt to see more clearly.

In the fairly recent past, the direct/indirect distinction in morals acquired an enormous importance in Catholic moral theology. For that reason, the effects of proportionalism are quite remarkable in that particular sphere. Some confusion has perhaps been caused by the number of points of view that have been aired in the debate regarding this distinction. We have seen, however, that most of those presented do not stand up to scrutiny. Although Knauer keeps the direct/indirect termi-

nology, the actual distinction between direct and indirect acting or intending has no real role to play in his theory. Grisez too seems to be on
the wrong track with his talk of directly turning against a basic good.
Apart from the fact that he appears to be dealing with moral goodness
and badness instead of the moral rightness or wrongness of actions, it
must be said that here too the direct/indirect distinction has no real role
to play. What the agent must not do is turn against a basic good. No
adverb is needed. McCormick's need to resort to his necessary connection
theory would appear to be caused by his falling under the influence of
the illusion of the incommensurability of goods or values. The basic goods,
he says, are incommensurable, but they are associated.[2] The reader will
remember that we have already seen McCormick stating that we do in
fact commensurate.[3] Here, however, he states that, while it is possible
to weigh some goods against each other, it is not possible to do so where
basic goods are concerned. The moment we see the error in claiming
incommensurability, the need for McCormick's necessary connection requirement disappears. As we have seen, moreover, it does not stand up
to close examination, and McCormick himself does not claim to be totally
convinced about its validity.

Although, however, McCormick's necessary connection requirement
would appear to be both unnecessary and unfounded, his misgivings about
Schüller's drastic reduction of the sphere of usefulness of the direct/indirect
distinction may be justified if we take into account indirect consequences
which are improbable or perhaps totally unforeseen. The agent takes into
account all foreseeable consequences (including improbable ones) and sees
that he has a proportionate reason for his proposed act, which he thereupon
performs. An indirect evil effect which was either seen to be highly
improbable or was not foreseen at all renders the reason for the act quite
inadequate. The agent is obviously less responsible for that effect than
for the more direct ones. It may be objected that the important factor
here is neither directness nor indirectness, but improbability or the fact
that the effect was unforeseen. However, the direct/indirect distinction
would appear to have some relevance here. After all, direct consequences
(if we adopt Selling's definition of "direct") cannot be considered improbable, and it is highly unlikely (although perhaps not impossible) that
they would be unforeseen in a free and fully conscious act.

Perhaps the most important criticism aimed at proportionalism is that
aired by Connery, among others, concerning the burden it places on the
shoulders of the agent. The reader will remember that, in distinguishing
proportionalism from consequentialism, we pointed out that the agent

must take into account not only the so-called welfare values, but also dignity values, expressive actions, institutional obligations, the meaning of the action, the premoral evil of breaking a promise, the unfairness of a situation, etc. We also suggested that a list of rules of preference like that prepared by Ginters might be useful to the agent trying to work out which is the greater good or the greater evil in cases of conflict. This might seem to leave the agent with quite a complicated "calculation" to do, at least in certain difficult cases of conflict. Now, the psychologist Lawrence Kohlberg informs us that, according to the results of extensive research conducted by him and his colleagues, most adults never succeed in rising above the conventional level in their moral reasoning. Is Connery right, then, in fearing that too much is expected of the agent?

The immediate answer that comes to mind is that one or two of the so-called "traditional" principles demand even more. The principle of double effect (which includes the need for a proportionate reason) is perhaps the most obvious example. Such an answer, however, does not make the problem go away. Most of the time the agent experiences no great difficulty because the rightness or wrongness of most actions is sufficiently evident. However, there will be difficult cases of conflict in the lives of all of us. Obviously, a person who has never succeeded in rising above the level of what is conventional is not well equipped to deal with such situations. This alone, however, is no reason for abandoning proportionalism, any more than, on its own, it is a reason for abandoning the principles of double effect and totality. It does most certainly point to the need for more research. Here, therefore, we must begin to think about the need to widen the debate on proportionalism. An enormous problem seems to exist at the level of moral education. Clearly, there is scope, and indeed a need, for dialogue with psychologists here. Just how can an ethics of individual responsibility (which proportionalism is) be communicated to people at large, and how can they become capable of applying it?

Connected to the problem of the burden placed on the individual's shoulders is the problem of subjectivism, a fear of which seems to be at the root of some of the difficulties envisioned by some opponents of proportionalism.[4] Proportionalism puts the onus on the moral subject. There is nothing strange in that. Only a totally deontological ethics of blind obedience could do otherwise. Leaving the subject to make his or her own responsible judgments, moreover, is not the same as subjectivism. On the other hand, it must be admitted that proportionalism is open to abuse in a subjectivistic way, just as the principle of totality, the principle of double effect, and just about any other principle one cares to mention are open to abuse. If, moreover, those deontological norms we discussed earlier are abandoned, proportionalism has a wider field of application than those principles.

First, it should be pointed out that any problems arising from the badness of the agent cannot be cured by a system, a principle or a deontological norm. Love is lacking. The bad person will do what he wants when he wants regardless of the norms accepted by his good fellow men, although he might hypocritically claim to have a proportionate reason for his action in order to make himself look good in the eyes of his fellow men. Who knows how many wars have been "justified" in that way?

However, the fear of subjectivism is not so easily dismissed. It may reasonably be supposed that some people will sometimes just make mistakes. They will not find (and will perhaps not even be capable of finding) what is objectively the right thing to do in a particular situation. They will find only what seems to them to be the right thing to do. Obviously, this problem could not be overcome by a return to the so-called "traditional" principles because they too demand a proportionate reason and, in practice, impose a more complicated "calculation" on the agent than proportionalism does. Neither would the problem be solved by having recourse to deontological norms of behavior. As those norms do not have the universal validity they are sometimes thought to have, their indiscriminate use would also lead to morally wrong acts. It is, moreover, highly unlikely that the imposition of taboos on people (who must blindly conform) will in any way help them to rise above the level of conventional morality.

In other words, no steps backward will resolve the problem of subjectivism. However, there would appear to be no grounds for being totally satisfied with what the debate on proportionalism has provided in this sphere. Again we see that the debate must be widened and further developed. The aim must be not only to convince one's opponents (theologians and philosophers, for the most part) of the validity of proportionalism. One must also find ways to put it within the grasp of ordinary people, who may then use it to find what is really (objectively) right. In order to do this we need to go deeper than the usual descriptions of proportionalism. It is not enough to say that the proportionalist takes up the raw material: premoral goods—like health, a roof over one's head, nourishment, sensual pleasure, the value of a promise, etc.—and premoral evils—like sickness, the destruction of someone's house, starvation, sensual pain, the unfairness of a situation, etc.—and then weighs them against each other, thereby discovering the rightness or wrongness of the proposed act. We need to ask how we come to acquire knowledge about the accumulated wisdom of mankind regarding premoral goods and evils and acts which are described in very general terms as usually right or usually wrong—a question the answer to which is perhaps not so easily obtained as one might at first think. We then need to ask how the individual at various stages in his or her life learns to appreciate goods, rightness, etc., How is his or her freedom impaired? How do people grow in appreciation and freedom? Assuming that a good measure of such appreciation and freedom is achieved, how does the individual set about comparing the various premoral goods and evils in a particular situation? What processes are involved? What we are really asking is: how does a person arrive at knowledge of objective rightness? It would, of course, be folly to assume that no scholars have begun research in these areas. There is no call for proportionalists to start from scratch. Again, dialogue with other scholars is called for.

Our analysis has, I think, demonstrated clearly enough the coherence and validity of proportionalism. It has, however, been developed at a point in time in which scholars in other disciplines have made somewhat depressing discoveries about the present state of mankind. Most people, it seems, would, in difficult situations of conflict, find it extremely difficult, perhaps impossible, to arrive with any degree of certainty at the objectively right solution, and many of them would accept whatever solution was suggested by convention or an "authority." The debate must therefore be widened, not only to give a deeper anthropological, episte-mological and metaphysical basis to the theory of proportionalism, but also so that the enormous problem of moral education may be tackled. If we are satisfied that proportionalism is *what* must be taught, we must now ask *how* it is to be taught.

Too much time has been spent going around in circles, repeating the same things, because a situation of near deadlock has existed in the debate on proportionalism for several years. To some extent, this has been caused by mistakes made on both sides and by misunderstandings. That is to be expected. When new ideas are produced scholars are often working in the dark, at least to some extent. Now, however, that some twenty years have passed since the debate got under way, and the advantage of hindsight is available, it is time to take a dispassionate look back over those years to see what has been achieved, how it has been achieved, what mistakes have been made, how they can be overcome, etc. This I have endeavored to do. I hope that I have made some contribution towards breaking the deadlock and that my efforts will provide some illumination for the future progress of the debate.

Notes

1. J. Ratzinger, "Dissent and Proportionalism in Moral Theology," *Origins* (March 1984): 668.

2. R.A. McCormick, *Notes . . . 1965 through 1980*, 719.

3. See Chapter Five, notes 77 and 78.

4. Perhaps the most obvious example is B.M. Kiely. See his "The Impracticality of Proportionalism," *Gregorianum* 66 (1985): 655–86.

Bibliography

Alonso, V. 1937. *El principio del doble efecto en los comentadores de Santo Tomaso de Aquino desde Cayetano hasta los Salmanticences. Explicación del derecho de defensa según Santo Tomaso de Aquino.* Rome.

Aquinas, St. Thomas. *Summa Theologiae II, II.*

Attard, Mark. 1976. *Compromise in Morality.* Rome: Institutum Carmelitanum.

Böckle, Franz. 1976. "Glaube und Handeln." *Concilium* 120: 641–47.

Bright, Laurence. 1965. Introduction to *Love and Fertility,* by W. van der Marck. London: Sheed and Ward.

Broad, C.D. 1930. *Five Types of Ethical Theory.* London: Routledge and Kegan Paul.

Cahill, Lisa Sowle. 1981. "Teleology, Utilitarianism, and Christian Ethics," *Theological Studies* 42: 601–29.

Chiavacci, Enrico. 1976. *Teologia Morale.* Vol. 1, *Morale Generale.* Assisi: Cittadella Editrice.

Chirico, Peter. 1967. "Tension, Morality and Birth Control." *Theological Studies* 28: 258–85.

———. 1970. "Morality in General and Birth Control in Particular." *Chicago Studies* 9: 19–33.

———. 1983. *Infallibility. The Crossroads of Doctrine.* Wilmington, Del.: Michael Glazier.

Composta, Dario. 1981. "Il consequenzialismo. Una nuova corrente della 'nuova morale'." *Divinitas* 25: 127–56.

Connell, Francis J. 1953. *Outlines of Moral Theology.* Milwaukee: Bruce.

Connery, John R. 1977. *Abortion: The Development of the Roman Catholic Perspective.* Chicago: Loyola University Press.

———. 1979. "Morality of Consequences: A Critical Appraisal." In Curran and McCormick, eds. (1979a: 244–66).

————. 1981. "Catholic Ethics: Has the Norm for Rule-Making Changed?" *Theological Studies* 42: 232–50.

————. 1983. "The Teleology of Proportionate Reason." *Theological Studies* 44: 489–96.

Corish, Patrick J. 1981. *The Catholic Community in the Seventeenth and Eighteenth Centuries.* Dublin: Helicon Ltd.

Coventry, John. 1966. "Christian Conscience." *The Heythrop Journal* 7: 145–60.

Crotty, Nicholas. 1971. "Conscience and Conflict." *Theological Studies* 32: 208–32.

Curran, Charles E. 1968a. "Absolute Norms and Medical Ethics." In *Absolutes in Moral Theology?*, edited by Charles E. Curran. Washington, D.C.: Corpus.

————. 1968b. "Dialogue with Joseph Fletcher." In *A New Look at Christian Morality.* 159–75. Notre Dame, Ind.: Fides.

————. 1970. "Is There a Distinctively Christian Social Ethic?" In *Metropolis: Christian Presence and Responsibility,* edited by P.D. Morris. Notre Dame, Ind.: Fides.

————. 1972. "Dialogue with the Future: Roman Catholic Theology in the United States Faces the Seventies," in *Catholic Moral Theology in Dialogue.* Notre Dame and London: University of Notre Dame Press.

————. 1975. "Divorce in the Light of a Revised Moral Theology," in *Ongoing Revisions: Studies in Moral Theology.* 66–106. Notre Dame, Ind.: Fides.

————. 1979. "Utilitarianism and Contemporary Moral Theology: Situating the Debates." In Curran and McCormick, eds. (1979a: 341–62).

Curran, Charles E., and Richard A. McCormick, eds. 1979a. *Readings in Moral Theology No. 1: Moral Norms and Catholic Tradition.* New York: Paulist Press.

————. 1979b. *Readings in Moral Theology No. 2: The Distinctiveness of Christian Ethics.* New York: Paulist Press.

————. 1982. *Readings in Moral Theology No. 3: The Magisterium and Morality.* New York: Paulist Press.

Dailey, Robert H. 1970. *Introduction to Moral Theology.* New York: Bruce.

Dedek, John F. 1968. "Freedom of the Catholic Conscience." *Chicago Studies* 7: 115–25.

————. 1972. *Human Life, Some Moral Issues.* New York: Sheed and Ward.

————. 1977. "Moral Absolutes in the Predecessors of St. Thomas." *Theological Studies* 38: 654–80.

————. 1979. "Intrinsically Evil Acts: An Historical Study of the Mind of St. Thomas." *The Thomist* 43: 385–413.

————. 1983. "Intrinsically Evil Act. The Emergence of a Doctrine." *Recherches de théologie ancienne et médiévale* 50: 191–226.

Deidun, Thomas. 1981. *New Covenant Morality in Paul*. Rome: Biblical Institute Press.

Di Ianni, Albert M. 1979. "The Direct/Indirect Distinction in Morals." In Curran and McCormick, eds. (1979a: 215–43).

Ermecke, Gustav. 1974. "Das Problem der Universalität oder Allgemeingültigkeit sittlicher Normen innerweltlicher Lebensgestaltung." *Münchener theologische Zeitschrift* 25: 18–33.

Farraher, Joseph. 1963. "Notes on Moral Theology." *Theological Studies* 24: 53–105.

Finnis, John M. 1970. "Natural Law and Unnatural Acts." *The Heythrop Journal* 11: 365–87.

————. 1973. "The Rights and Wrongs of Abortion." *Philosophy and Public Affairs* 2.

————. 1980. *Natural Law and Natural Rights*. Oxford: Clarendon Press.

Fletcher, Joseph. 1966. *Situation Ethics*. Philadelphia: Westminster.

Foot, Philippa. 1967. Introduction to *Theories of Ethics*, edited by Philippa Foot. Oxford: Oxford University Press.

Ford, John C., and Germain Grisez. 1978. "Contraception and the Infallibility of the Ordinary Magisterium." *Theological Studies* 39: 258–312.

Frankena, William K. 1967. "The Naturalistic Fallacy." In *Theories of Ethics*, edited by Philippa Foot. Oxford: Oxford University Press.

————. 1978. "McCormick and the Traditional Distinction." In McCormick and Ramsey, eds. (1978: 145–64).

Fuchs, Josef. 1970. "Human, Humanist and Christian Morality," in *Human Values and Christian Morality*. Dublin: Gill and Macmillan.

————. 1971. "Moral Aspects of Human Progress," in *Theology Meets Progress*, edited by P. Land. 145–69. Rome: Gregorian University Press.

————. 1974. "Sittliche Normen—Universalien und Generalisierungen." *Münchener theologische Zeitschrift* 25: 18–33.

————. 1979. "Is There a Specifically Christian Morality?" In Curran and McCormick, eds. (1979b: 3–19).

———. 1980. "The 'Sin of the World' and Normative Morality." *Gregorianum* 61: 51–75.

———. 1981. *Essere del Signore.* Rome: Gregorian University.

———. 1983. "The Absoluteness of Behavioral Moral Norms." In: *Personal Responsibility and Christian Morality.* Washington, D.C.: Georgetown University Press, and Dublin: Gill and Macmillan. 115–52.

———. 1984a. "Teaching Morality: The Tension between Bishops and Theologians within the Church." In *Christian Ethics in a Secular Arena.* Washington, D.C.: Georgetown University Press, and Dublin: Gill and Macmillan. 131–53.

———. 1984b. "Moral Truths—Truths of Salvation?" In *Christian Ethics in a Secular Arena.* Washington, D.C.: Georgetown University Press, and Dublin: Gill and Macmillan. 48–67.

———. 1984c. "An Ongoing Discussion in Christian Ethics: 'Intrinsically Evil Acts'?" In: *Christian Ethics in a Secular Arena.* Washington, D.C.: Georgetown University Press, and Dublin: Gill and Macmillan. 71–90.

———. 1984d. "Das Gottesbild und die Moral innerweltlichen Handelns." *Stimmen der Zeit* 202: 363–82.

Gaffney, James, 1983. "On Parenesis and Fundamental Moral Theology." *Journal of Religious Ethics* 11: 23–34.

Ghoos, J. 1951. "L'acte à double effet. Etude de théologie positive." *Ephemerides Theologicae Lovanienses* 27: 30–52.

Ginters, Rudolf. 1982. *Werte und Normen: Einführung in die philosophische und theologische Ethik.* Dusseldorf: Wandenhoeck und Ruprecht.

Grisez, Germain. 1970. *Abortion: The Myths, the Realities and the Arguments.* New York: Corpus.

———. 1981. "Christian Moral Theology and Consequentialism." In *Principles of Catholic Moral Life.* Washington, D.C.

———. 1983. *The Way of the Lord Jesus.* Vol. 1, *Christian Moral Principles.* Chicago: Franciscan Herald Press.

———. 1985. "Infallibility and Specific Moral Norms: A Review Discussion. *The Thomist* 49: 248–87.

Grisez, Germain, and Joseph M. Boyle, Jr. 1979. *Life and Death with Liberty and Justice.* Notre Dame and London: University of Notre Dame Press.

Grisez, Germain, and Russell Shaw. 1974. *Beyond the New Morality.* Notre Dame and London: University of Notre Dame Press.

Hallett, Garth. 1983. *Christian Moral Reasoning: An Analytic Guide.* Notre Dame and London: University of Notre Dame Press.

Hare, R.M. 1952. *The Language of Morals*. Oxford: Clarendon Press.

Häring, Bernard. 1969. "Dynamism and Continuity in a Personalistic Approach to Natural Law." In *Norm and Context in Christian Ethics*, edited by Gene H. Outka and Paul Ramsey. London. 199–218.

———. 1972. *Medical Ethics*. Slough, England: St. Paul Publications.

Heenan, John C. 1968. "The Authority of the Church." *The Tablet* 222: 488–90.

Hill, John P. 1976. *The Ethics of G.E. Moore: A New Interpretation*. Assen: Van Gorcum.

Hughes, John Jay. 1971. "Infallible? An Inquiry Considered." *Theological Studies* 32: 183–207.

Hughes, Philip. 1954. *The Reformation in England*. London: Hollis and Carter.

Hurley, Denis E. 1966. "A New Moral Principle—When Right and Duty Clash." *The Furrow* 17: 619–22.

Janssens, Louis. 1977. "Norms and Priorities in a Love Ethic." *Louvain Studies* 6 (September): 207–38.

———. 1979. "Ontic Evil and Moral Evil." In Curran and McCormick, eds. (1979a: 40–93).

———. 1982. "St. Thomas and the Question of Proportionality." *Louvain Studies* 9: 26–46.

Johnson, Oliver A. 1959. *Rightness and Goodness*. The Hague: M. Nijhoff.

Johnstone, Brian V. 1985. "The Meaning of Proportionate Reason in Contemporary Moral Theology." *The Thomist* 49: 223–47.

Jossua, J.P. 1971. "Moral Theology Forum: The Fidelity of Love and the Indissolubility of Christian Marriage." *The Clergy Review* 56: 172–81.

Kaiser, Robert B. 1985. "The Long Road to Birth Control Control." *National Catholic Reporter* 21. 27: 9–11.

Keane, Philip S. 1977. *Sexual Morality: A Catholic Perspective*. New York: Paulist Press.

———. 1982. "The Objective Moral Order: Reflections on Recent Research." *Theological Studies* 43: 260–78.

Kelly, Gerald. 1953. "Notes on Moral Theology, 1952." *Theological Studies* 14: 31–72.

Kiely, Bartholomew M. 1985. "The Impracticality of Proportionalism." *Gregorianum* 66: 655–86.

Knauer, Peter. 1965. "La détermination du bien et du mal moral par le principe du double effet." *Nouvelle Revue Théologique* 87: 356–76. (A shortened English version was published as "The Principle of the Double Effect" in *Theology Digest* 15 (1967): 100–04).

———. 1979. "The Hermeneutic Function of the Principle of Double Effect." In Curran and McCormick, eds. (1979a: 1–39).

———. 1980. "Fundamentalethik: teleologische als deontologische Normenbegründung." *Theologie und Philosophie* 55: 321–60.

Koestler, Arthur. 1972. *The Roots of Coincidence.* London: Hutchinson and Co.

Komonchak, Joseph A. 1982. "Ordinary Papal Magisterium and Religious Assent." In Curran and McCormick, eds. (1982: 67–90).

Korsgaard, C.M. 1983. "Two Distinctions in Goodness." *The Philosophical Review* 92: 169–95.

Kovesi, Julius. 1984. "*Principia Ethica* Re-examined: The Ethics of a Proto-Logical Atomism." *Philosophy* 59: 157–70.

Kramer, Herbert G. 1935. *The Indirect Voluntary or Voluntarium in Causa.* Washington: Catholic University Press.

Langan, John. 1979. "Direct and Indirect—Some Recent Exchanges between Paul Ramsey and Richard McCormick." *Religious Studies Review* 5: 95–101.

Lewy, Casimir. 1970. "G.E. Moore on the Naturalistic Fallacy." In *G.E. Moore. Essays in Retrospect,* edited by A. Ambrose and M. Lazerowitz. London: George Allen and Unwin. 292–303.

Lonergan, Bernard. 1957. *Insight.* London: Darton Longman and Todd.

———. 1967. "The Transition from a Classicist World View to Historical Mindedness." In *Law for Liberty: The Role of Law in the Church Today,* edited by J.E. Biechler. Baltimore: Helicon Press.

———. 1973. *Method in Theology.* New York: Herder.

Maguire, Daniel C. 1968. "Morality and the Magisterium." *Cross Currents* 18: 41–65.

Mangan, J. 1949. "An Historical Analysis of the Principle of Double Effect." *Theological Studies* 10: 41–61.

May, William E. 1977. *Human Existence, Medicine and Ethics: Reflections on Human Life.* Chicago: Franciscan Herald Press.

———. 1982. "Church Teaching and the Immorality of Contraception." *Homiletic and Pastoral Review.* 82: 9–18.

———. 1984. "Aquinas and Janssens on the Moral Meaning of Human Acts." *The Thomist* 48: 566–606.

May, William E., and John F. Harvey. 1977. *On Understanding Human Sexuality.* Chicago: Franciscan Herald Press.

Mausbach, Joseph, and Gustav Ermecke. 1961. *Katholische Moraltheologie.* Vol. III. Münster: Westfalen.

McCarthy, John. 1960. *Problems in Theology, II: The Commandments.* Dublin: Browne and Nolan.

McCormick, Richard A. 1968a. "The New Morality." *America* 118: 769–72.

———. 1968b. "Past Church Teaching on Abortion." *Proceedings of the Catholic Theological Society of America* 23: 131–51.

———. 1969. "Teaching Role of the Magisterium and of Theologians." *Proceedings of the Catholic Theological Society of America* 24: 239–54.

———. 1973. *Ambiguity in Moral Choice*. Milwaukee: Marquette University.

———. 1976. "Il principio del duplice effetto." *Concilium* 12/10: 1723–43.

———. 1978. "A Commentary on the Commentaries." In McCormick and Ramsey, eds. (1978: 193–267).

———. 1981. *Notes on Moral Theology 1965 through 1980*. Lanham, Md.: University Press of America.

———. 1984. *Notes on Moral Theology 1981 through 1984*. Lanham, Md.: University Press of America.

———. 1985. "Notes on Moral Theology 1984." *Theological Studies* 46: 50–64.

McCormick, Richard A., and Paul Ramsey, eds. 1978. *Doing Evil to Achieve Good*. Chicago: Loyola University Press.

Milhaven, John Giles. 1966. "Towards an Epistemology of Ethics." *Theological Studies* 27: 228–41.

———. 1968. "Moral Absolutes and Thomas Aquinas." In Curran (1968a: 154–85).

———. 1970a. "A New Sense of Sin." *Critic* 28: 14–21.

———. 1970b. "The Abortion Debate: An Epistemological Interpretation." *Theological Studies* 81: 106–24.

———. 1971. "Objective Moral Evaluation of Consequences." *Theological Studies* 32: 407–30.

Milhaven, John Giles, and David J. Casey. 1967. "Introduction to the Theological Background to the New Morality." *Theological Studies* 28: 213–44.

Moore, George Edward. 1932. "Is Goodness a Quality?" *Aristotelian Society Proceedings*. Supp. Vol. II.

———. 1962. *The Commonplace Book 1919–1953*. Edited by Casimir Lewy. London: George Allen and Unwin.

———. 1965. *Principia Ethica*. Cambridge: Cambridge University Press.

———. 1966. *Ethics*. London: Oxford University Press.

Murtagh, James. 1973. *Intrinsic Evil*. Doctoral dissertation, Gregorian University, Rome.

152 / *Bernard Hoose*

Noonan, John T., Jr. 1965. *Contraception. A History of Its Treatment by the Catholic Theologians and Canonists.* Cambridge, Mass.: Harvard University Press.

O'Callaghan, Denis F. 1965. "May a Spy Take His Life?" *Irish Ecclesiastical Record* 103: 259–64.

O'Connell, Timothy E. 1975. "The Question of Moral Norms." *The American Ecclesiastical Review* 169: 377–88.

———. 1978. *Principles for a Catholic Morality.* New York: The Seabury Press.

Peters, B., T. Beemer, and C. Van der Poel. 1966. "Cohabitation in Marital State of Mind." *Homiletic and Pastoral Review* 66: 566–77.

Quay, Paul M. 1979. "Morality by Calculation of Values." In Curran and McCormick, eds. (1979a: 267–93).

———. 1985. "The Disvalue of Ontic Evil." *Theological Studies* 46: 262–86.

Ramsey, Paul. 1965. *Deeds and Rules in Christian Ethics.* London: Oliver and Boyd.

———. 1976. "Some Rejoinders." *Journal of Religious Ethics* 4: 185–237.

———. 1978. "Incommensurability and Indeterminacy in Moral Choice." In McCormick and Ramsey, eds. (1978: 69–144).

Ratzinger, Joseph. 1984. "Dissent and Proportionalism in Moral Theology." *Origins* (March): 666–69.

Rigali, Norbert J. 1981. "Evil and Models of Christian Ethics." *Horizons* 8: 7–22.

Robert, Charles. 1970. "La situation de 'conflit': un thème dangereux de la théologie morale d'aujourd'hui." *Revue des Sciences Religieuses* 44: 190–213.

Ross, William David. 1949. *Foundations of Ethics.* Oxford: The Clarendon Press.

———. 1937. "The Meaning of 'Good'." *Travaux du IXe Congrès International de Philosophie.* Vol. XI, Part II. 78–82.

Rossi, Leandro. 1972. "Il limite del principio del duplice effetto." *Rivista di Teologia Morale* 4: 11–37.

Schnackenburg, Rudolph. 1965. *The Moral Teaching of the New Testament.* New York: Herder and Herder.

Scholz, Franz. 1980. "Possibilità e impossibilità dell'agire indiretto." In *Fede cristiana e agire morale,* edited by K. Demmer and B. Schüller. Assisi: Cittadella Editrice. 289–311. (This is the Italian version of "Objekt und Umstande, Wesenswirkungen und Nebeneffekte." In:

Christlich Glauben und Handeln. 1977. Dusseldorf: Patmos Verlag. 243–60.)

Schüller, Bruno. 1967. "Can Moral Theology Ignore Natural Law?" *Theology Digest* 15: 94–99.

———. 1970. "Typen ethischer Argumentation in der Katholischen Moraltheologie." *Theologie und Philosophie* 45: 526–50.

———. 1971. "What Ethical Principles Are Universally Valid?" *Theology Digest* 19: 23–28. (This is an abridged version of "Zur Problematik allgemein verbindlicher ethischer Grundsätze." *Theologie und Philosophie* 45 (1970): 1–23).

———. 1974. "Neuere Beiträge zum Thema 'Begründung sittlicher Normen'." *Theologische Berichte 4.* Einsiedeln: Benziger. 109–81.

———. 1978a. "Die Personwürde des Menschen als Beweisgrund in der normativen Ethik." *Theologie und Glaube* 53: 538–55.

———. 1978b. "The Double Effect in Catholic Thought: A Reevaluation." In McCormick and Ramsey, eds. (1978: 165–91).

———. 1979a. "Direct Killing/Indirect Killing." In Curran and McCormick, eds. (1979a: 138–57).

———. 1979b. "Various Types of Grounding for Ethical Norms." In Curran and McCormick, eds. (1979a: 184–98).

———. 1980. *Die Begründung sittlicher Urteile. Typen ethischer Argumentation in der Moraltheologie.* Dusseldorf: Patmos Verlag.

———. 1983. "Zur Begründung sittlicher Normen." In *Der Mensch und sein sittlicher Auftrag,* edited by Heinz Altaus. Freiburg: Herder. 73–95.

Schultz, Janice L. 1985. "Is-Ought: Prescribing and a Present Controversy." *The Thomist* 49: 1–23.

Seifert, Josef. 1985. "Absolute Moral Obligations towards Finite Goods as Foundation of Intrinsically Right and Wrong Actions." *Anthropos* 1: 57–94.

Selling, Joseph A. 1980. "The Problem of Reinterpreting the Principle of Double Effect." *Louvain Studies* 8: 47–62.

Skrzydlewski, W.B. 1985. "Conflict and Schism in Moral Theology and Sexual Ethics." *Homiletic and Pastoral Review* 85: 23–32, 48–50. (This article was first published in the Polish review *Collectanea Theologica,* Warsaw 52 (1982). II: 5–38).

Smart, J.J.C. 1967. "Extreme and Restricted Utilitarianism." In *Theories of Ethics,* edited by P. Foot. Oxford: Oxford University Press.

Smith, William B. 1981. "The Revision of Moral Theology in Richard A. McCormick." *Homiletic and Pastoral Review* 81: 8–28.

Sullivan, Francis A. 1983. *Magisterium. Teaching Authority in the Catholic Church*. Dublin: Gill and Macmillan.

Thielicke, Helmut. 1966. *Theological Ethics, I: Foundations*. Philadelphia: Wm. B. Eerdmans.

Toulmin, Stephen E. 1950. *An Examination of the Place of Reason in Ethics*. Cambridge: Cambridge University Press.

Ugorji, Lucius I. 1985. *The Principle of Double Effect. A Critical Appraisal of Its Traditional Understanding and Its Modern Interpretation*. Frankfurt and New York: P. Lang.

Vacek, Edward. 1985. "Proportionalism: One View of the Debate." *Theological Studies* 46: 287–314.

Van der Marck, William. 1965. *Love and Fertility*. London: Sheed and Ward.

Van der Poel, Cornelius. 1968. "The Principle of Double Effect." In *Absolutes in Moral Theology?*, edited by C.E. Curran. Washington, D.C.: Corpus. 186–210.

Vaughan, Austin B. 1967. "The Role of the Ordinary Magisterium of the Universal Episcopate." *Proceedings of the Catholic Theological Society of America* 22: 1–19.

Walter, James J. 1984. "Proportionate Reason and Its Three Levels of Inquiry: Structuring the Ongoing Debate." *Louvain Studies* 10: 30–40.

Wrenn, Lawrence G. 1973. "Marriage—Indissoluble or Fragile?" In *Divorce and Remarriage in the Catholic Church*, edited by L.G. Wrenn. New York: Newman Press.

Index

An asterisk * indicates that the reference is to a note only.